Mayan Safari

THE LONGMAN SPANISH CULTURE SERIES

A Beginning
Spanish Reader

Mayan Safari

Aubrey Smith

Longman

Mayan Safari: A Beginning Spanish Reader

Longman, 95 Church Street, White Plains, N.Y. 10601

Associated companies:
Longman Group Ltd., London
Longman Cheshire Pty., Melbourne
Longman Paul Pty., Auckland
Copp Clark Pitman, Toronto

Credits: Figures on pages 141 and 142 are from
The First Book of the Ancient Maya by
Barbara Beck, pp. 29 & 30. © Copyright
Franklin Watts, Inc., 1965. Reproduced
with permission.

Executive editor: Lyn McLean
Development editor: Karen Davy
Production editor: Janice L. Baillie
Text design: NSG/Kevin Kall
Cover design: Joseph De Pinho
Cover illustration/photo: Pam Johnson
Text art: Pam Johnson

ISBN: 0-8013-0401-6

1 2 3 4 5 6 7 8 9 10-MA-9594939291

Contents

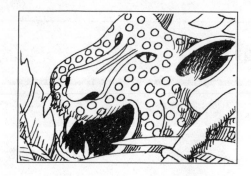

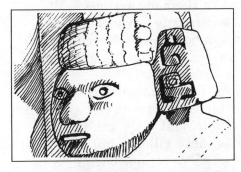

Introduction

Mayan Safari is a true adventure story in Spanish. It transports the student into the jungles of Mexico, Chiapas, and Yucatan in an exciting search for the Mayans. With a history of dramatic conflict and incredible achievements that culminated in their mysterious disappearance, the Mayans had an extraordinarily advanced civilization whose customs, rituals, and symbols can be traced back thousands of years through hieroglyphics, codices, and the *Popul Vuh* (Mayan bible).

Today, many descendents of the Mayans live in mountain villages of Chiapas and Central America, wear distinctive native dress, and still leave offerings in mountain caves to their ancient gods. In *Mayan Safari,* the Johnson family not only visits these villages but they also learn about Mayan gods and witchcraft at a mysterious curing ritual. Later, they descend the famous secret stairway to the hidden tomb of Pacal. Many other exciting adventures await them in Yucatan, where they find the Throne of the Red Jaguar, the Sacred Well, and the diving god of Tulum.

I went on this safari myself in 1989 and 1990. I climbed pyramids and temples, studied hieroglyphics, traced the designs on Indian **huipiles** back to the ancient symbols of the *Popul Vuh,* watched **curanderos** perform miracles, and attended carnival in a mountain village in Chiapas during the five days before Lent (the Mayan calendar had a month of only five days). I was privileged to observe tribal ceremonies that were accompanied by music of the harp, guitar, and violin, with melodies based on seventeenth-century madrigals.

Mayan Safari is a great *motivator* because it involves the student in an exciting, visual, tactile, true adventure story in one of the most fascinating, mysterious countries in the world—Mexico!

There are twenty-seven chapters in *Mayan Safari*. Chapter features are:

ANTES DE LEER (Prereading exercises). This section, presented in the first twenty chapters, introduces the student to special skills and strategies that can be used to improve reading skills. Included in this section are discussions of cognates, punctuation, idiomatic expressions, and word families. The student gains insight and focus that will enable him or her to read the story with greater confidence and comprehension.

THE ADVENTURE STORY. An episode of the adventures of the Johnson family.

ACTIVIDADES. A variety of activities challenge the student:

1. Questions based on the story
2. True/false
3. Matching words and phrases
4. Translations
5. Sentence completion
6. Choosing the right connotation
7. Creating original sentences, both written and oral
8. Research projects
9. Art projects (drawing, painting, clay modeling, painting murals, etc.)

¿SABES? This section, at the end of the odd-numbered chapters, contains fascinating linguistic and cultural information that will enhance the student's journey in search of the Mayans. The Latin and Arabic roots of the Spanish language are presented as clues to deciphering unfamiliar words. Also included in this section are interesting Spanish connections to Roman mythology, body and sign language, Mayan gods, the mysteries of witchcraft, tomb treasures, and the language of today's Mayans.

DESAFÍO (Challenge). The student is challenged to create the *essence* of the adventure story in a variety of art forms: in paint, clay, papier mâché, in dramatization, or on paper as a research project. Learning is reinforced both visually and tactily. Many classes have created entire Mayan villages with pyramids, hieroglyphic stelaes, Indians in native dress weaving, making pottery, or playing a Mayan ball game. Some students have even re-created the ritual of human and animal sacrifice in clay!

Mayan Safari is a very exciting, motivational journey into the Spanish language, into archaeology, and into the culture of ancient and modern Mexico.

Additional Ideas for Student Involvement

1. Map-making. The making of ordinary or bas-relief maps offers many opportunities for students to learn geography, anthropology, archaeology, and sociology. Individual research projects challenge the student to delve into subjects of particular interest, such as the flora and fauna of a region, native customs and costumes, witchcraft, and comparison with other cultures around the world.

2. Creating an entire Mayan village in clay, papier mâché or on mural paper is a wonderful class project, with each student choosing his or her particular area of interest to transform into some art form. In schools where "core curriculum" is emphasized, students from history, geography, anthropology, and art classes could also participate in this project, each adding a new dimension to the overall understanding of the Mayans. Student explanations in Spanish of the Mayan village to other Spanish classes will further reinforce the verbal, visual, and tactile impact of this project.

3. Making puppets for dramatization of student-written versions of the story. Making indigenous clothing and headdresses of gods and chieftains.

4. Hieroglyphics. Students could create their own language of symbols and picture-writing, after which they could construct stelaes of papier mâché that convey their story. They could make accordion-pleated **codices** similar to the three existing codices, the only written/drawn Mayan chronicles not destroyed by the Spaniards.

5. Dramatizations: The Aztec Empire—Tenochtitlan   Chap. 15
Dr. Caso's discovery of Monte Albán   Chap. 21
El Cañón del Sumidero   Chap. 22
San Juan de Chamula-witchcraft   Chap. 24
Palenque—Pacal's tomb. Class
artists could re-create the
sarcophagus   Chap. 25
Chichén Itzá—The Sacred Well   Chap. 26
The arrival of the Spaniards   Chap. 27

6. Research projects. The Mayans living today. Religious and social
conflicts. Political persecution. Genocide of Indian populations
in Central America. Rain forests being destroyed by land-hungry
developers. The current deciphering of Mayan hieroglyphics.
Comparison of Mayan pyramids/cultures with those of Egypt and
the Ziggurats. Religious and burial practices among indigenous
people the world over. Comparison of Creation Myths.

Dedication and Acknowledgments

This book is lovingly dedicated to my adventurous children, Katherine and Peter, and to my late husband, A. O. Smith, who cheerfully put up with my periodic disappearances into the jungle in search of indigenous cultures.

To Betty Buck, Annette Raphel, Linda Stikeleather and Marcia Trook, the creative spirits behind the Saturday Course, a special thanks for allowing me to convert the Milton Academy basement into a Mayan jungle and to lead hundreds of students into a new world where learning was clothed in imagination and fact disguised as fantasy.

Mil gracias to Harriet Dickson, Jackie McClellan, Anna Colbert, Adan Negrete, Ed Siegfried, Monica Posada, Karen Davy, and Janice Baillie, Mark Davies, and Pam Johnson, all of whom contributed in a variety of important ways to the book. To colleagues Leo Maza, chairman of the Modern Language Department at Milton Academy, and Marisol Maura, special words of appreciation for their support and expert evaluation of the text, with special emphasis on regional uses and connotations of Spanish.

The author would also like to give a loud ¡Olé! to Lyn McLean at Longman, whose wisdom, expertise, and enthusiasm from the beginning to the end of this project were greatly appreciated.

La familia Johnson

El señor Johnson

La señora Johnson

Catalina

Pedro

La tía Amalia

CAPÍTULO

El plan del viaje

1

Antes de leer

Cognates

It is fun to spot Spanish words that look and sound familiar, and remind you of words in English. These related words are called *cognates*. Words such as **exótico, fantástico, futuro,** and **misterioso** have the same meaning as their English equivalents, but have a Spanish pronunciation.

Draw a line to match each Spanish word in Column A with its English **cognado** *in Column B.*

A	B
1. capítulo	**a.** animals
2. interesante	**b.** ferocious
3. expresión	**c.** chapter
4. animales	**d.** interesting
5. feroces	**e.** expression

El plan del viaje°

"¿Un safari a las selvas° de México? ¿En busca de° los mayas? ¡Qué peligroso!"° exclama Amalia, la tía° de Catalina y Pedro.

"¿Peligroso? ¡No! ¡Emocionante!"° responde
5 Catalina con entusiasmo.

"El mundo° de los mayas es extraño° y misterioso. También en las selvas de México hay animales feroces, insectos carnívoros y aves° exóticas", explica Catalina, muy
10 entusiasmada.

"¡Qué horror!" grita° Amalia, con una expresión de miedo.°

viaje:	*trip*
selvas:	*jungles* • En busca de: *In search of* • peligroso: *dangerous*
tía:	*aunt*
Emocionante:	*Exciting*
mundo:	*world* • extraño: *strange*
aves:	*birds*
grita:	*shouts*
miedo:	*fear*

Actividades

A. ¿Sí o no? Write **sí** if the sentence is true according to the story. If the sentence is false, write **no;** then rewrite the sentence by correcting the underlined words.

1. Catalina y Pedro viajan a <u>California</u> en busca de los <u>incas</u>.

   No. Catalina y Pedro viajan a México en busca de los mayas.

2. Amalia es la <u>mamá</u> de Pedro.

3. Hay animales <u>misteriosos</u> en la selva.

_____

4. También hay <u>insectos carnívoros</u>.

_____

5. Las aves de la selva son <u>peligrosas</u>.

_____

B. ¿a, b o c? Circle the correct answer.

1. Exclama (line 3) probably means

  a. explains.

  b. excuses.

  c. exclaims.

2. Entusiasmo (line 5) probably means

  a. enthusiastic.

  b. enthusiasm.

  c. enthusiastically.

3. Insectos carnívoros (line 8) are probably

  a. insects found in carnivals.

  b. insects that smell like carnations.

  c. insects that are carnivorous.

4. ¡Qué horror! (line 11) probably means

  a. How exciting!

  b. How horrible!

  c. How strange!

¿Sabes?

Be a word detective! Many of the Spanish words that you will learn on this safari have Latin roots. The English, French, and Italian languages also have Latin roots. If you know a little Latin, it will be fun for you to solve word mysteries by identifying the roots of the words.

Por ejemplo *(For example): Carnis* in Latin means "flesh, meat." **Carne** in Spanish has the same meaning. Therefore, what would **carnívoros** probably mean? What thoughts come to mind when you see the words *carnival* and *reincarnation*?

Desafío *(Challenge).* Using both English and Spanish dictionaries, who can find the most words that have the Latin root *carn*? Find their meanings too!

CAPÍTULO

Pirámides y cuevas

2

Antes de leer

Question Words

Explorers going on a jungle safari need to ask a lot of questions. Here are some important question words that will help you.

¿adónde?	where (to)	¿Adónde va la familia?	*Where is the family going?*
¿cómo?	how what . . . like	¿Cómo estás? *How are you?*	
¿dónde?	where	¿Dónde están los mayas? *Where are the Mayas?*	
¿qué?	what	¿Qué es un insecto carnívoro? *What is a carnivorous insect?*	
¿quién?	who	¿Quién es Pedro? *Who is Pedro?*	
¿quiénes?	who (plural)	¿Quiénes son los Johnson? *Who are the Johnsons?*	

¡OJO! (*Look out!*) A Spanish question begins with an upside-down question mark (¿) and ends with a regular question mark (?). All question words carry an accent mark (').

Complete each of the following sentences with an appropriate question word from above. Read both the question and the answer before you decide what word is missing. Be sure to use the upside-down question mark, and don't forget the accent mark!

1. ___¿Cómo___ es el mundo de los mayas?
   Es extraño y misterioso.

2. _____ es Amalia?
   Es la tía de Catalina y Pedro.

3. _____ grita la tía Amalia?
   Grita "¡Qué horror!"

4. _____ hay en la selva?
   Hay animales feroces y aves exóticas.

5. _____ son indios misteriosos?
   Los mayas son indios misteriosos.

Pirámides y cuevas°

cuevas: *caves*

"Y también en la selva hay pirámides altas° y cuevas siniestras, con tesoros° y murciélagos!"° exclama Pedro, el hermano° de Catalina. Pedro y Catalina son
5 aventureros. Son exploradores como sus padres.°

¡Pirámides altas! ¡Animales feroces! ¡Cuevas con murciélagos! ¡Insectos carnívoros, como arañas,° tarántulas y
10 alacranes!° ¡No me digas!° ¡La familia Johnson está completamente loca!°

altas: *tall* • tesoros: *treasures*
murciélagos: *bats* • hermano: *brother*

padres: *parents*

arañas: *spiders*

alacranes: *scorpions* • ¡No me digas!: *You don't say!*
loca: *crazy*

Actividades

A. Preguntas *(Questions)*. Answer these questions

1. ¿Qué hay en la selva?
2. ¿Cómo son las pirámides?
3. ¿Quiénes son aventureros?
4. ¿Dónde están los murciélagos?
5. ¿Cómo está la familia Johnson?

B. En busca de cognados. There are some new cognates in the story. Find them, write them below, and give their English equivalents. The first letter of each cognate is given to help you spot them!

p_____   e_____

s_____   t_____

a_____   c_____

C. ¡Dibujemos! *(Let's draw!)*

un pirámide

un murciélago

una araña

una cueva

una selva

CAPÍTULO

Los preparativos

3

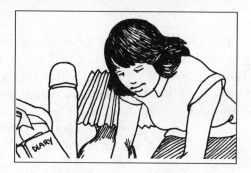

Antes de leer

Getting Meaning from Context

When you read, in English as well as in Spanish, you often run into words that you do not know. Most of the time, you can figure out the general meaning of a word by its context, or how it is used in the sentence.

Read these sentences and see if you can figure out the meaning of the underlined words.

1. El viaje a México no es <u>aburrido</u>; es muy interesante.
2. A Catalina le gusta <u>jugar</u> al béisbol.
3. La familia Johnson <u>escucha</u> música mexicana en la radio.

Los preparativos

Toda la familia está muy entusiasmada con los preparativos para el viaje. El señor y la señora Johnson preparan la ropa° para hacer las maletas.° Catalina y Pedro buscan la cámara para sacar fotos.

5 También buscan los binoculares para ver mejor° las aves y los animales de la selva. Buscan sus diarios porque planean escribir cada° día de sus aventuras en México.

"Papá, ¿tenemos una navaja?"° pregunta Pedro de

10 repente.°

ropa: *clothes* • hacer las maletas: *pack the suitcases*
mejor: *better*

cada: *each*

navaja: pocket *knife* • de repente: *suddenly*

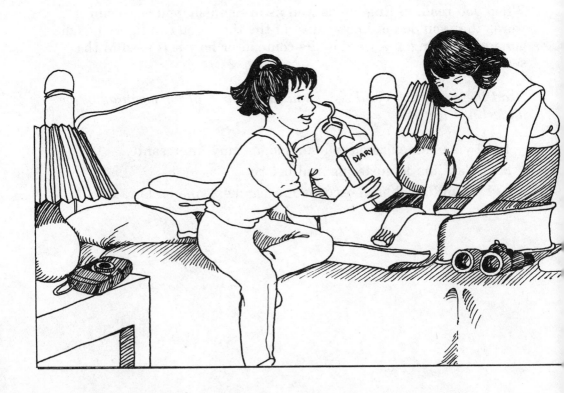

"¿Para qué necesitamos una navaja, Pedro?" contesta su papá.

"Para protección contra los jaguares", responde Pedro.

15 Pedro imagina los dientes° enormes, los ojos° siniestros y las garras fuertes° de los jaguares que esperan° en la oscuridad° de la selva.

dientes: *teeth* • ojos: *eyes*
garras fuertes: *strong claws* • esperan: *wait*
oscuridad: *darkness*

Actividades

A. Preguntas. Answer these questions

1. ¿Por qué está entusiasmada la familia Johnson?
2. ¿Qué preparan los Johnson?
3. ¿Qué hay en las maletas?
4. ¿Con qué van a ver los animales?
5. En la imaginación de Pedro, ¿cómo son los jaguares?

B. ¿a, b o c? Circle the correct answer.

1. **Sacar fotos** (line 4) probably means
   a. to show pictures.
   b. to take pictures.
   c. to draw pictures.

2. **Ver** (line 5) probably means
   a. to carry.
   b. to kill.
   c. to see.

3. **Pregunta** (line 9) probably means
   a. says.
   b. shouts.
   c. asks.

4. **Contesta** (line 12) probably means the same as
   a. **exclama**.
   b. **responde**.
   c. **pregunta**.

5. **Contra** (line 13) probably means
   a. among.
   b. under.
   c. against.

C. ¡Identifica! Underline the part of the sentence from the story that helped you get the meaning of each of the words below. There may be more than one clue in each group.

1. sacar fotos:	buscan	cámara	para
2. ver:	binoculares	mejor	selva
3. pregunta:	de repente	Pedro	¿?

4. contesta: papá   pregunta   ¿para qué?

5. contra: responde   para   protección

D. ¿Para qué sirve? *(What's it used for?)* Draw a line to match each object in Column A to its use in Column B.

A	B
1. la navaja	**a.** la ropa
2. las maletas	**b.** escribir de las aventuras
3. la cámara	**c.** protección
4. los diarios	**d.** ver las aves y los animales
5. los binoculares	**e.** sacar fotos

¿Sabes?

The Latin word for *eye* is *oculus.* The Spanish word is **ojo.** The "eye family" has many recognizable members.

monóculos	*Mono* means "one" or "single" in Latin. Can you guess the meanings of **monóculo** and **monólogo**?
binoculares	*Bi* means "twice" or "two" in Latin. Therefore, what does **binoculares** mean?
ocultar	**Ocultar** means *to conceal.* The world of the occult is the hidden world, the unseen!

Knowing that **ojo** means *eye,* find the meanings of **ojera, ojialegre,** and **ojituerto.** Then _____, draw them!

CAPÍTULO

La navaja

4

Antes de leer

Tener

There are many common expressions, or idioms, in Spanish that use the verb **tener** (*to have*). When **tener** is used in certain English expressions, it means *to be*.

tener calor	to be hot
tener cuidado	to be careful
tener frío	to be cold
tener hambre	to be hungry
tener miedo	to be afraid
tener prisa	to be in a hurry
tener razón	to be right
tener sueño	to be sleepy
tener suerte	to be lucky
tener _____ años	to be _____ years old

Tener is an irregular verb. It is conjugated as follows:

yo	tengo
tú	tienes
él	
ella }	tiene
usted	
nosotros, -as	tenemos
ellos	
ellas }	tienen
ustedes	

Complete these sentences with the correct form of **tener**.

1. Pedro _____ razón. Los jaguares son peligrosos.

2. "Yo no _____ miedo de los animales salvajes", grita

   Catalina.

3. Pedro y su papá _____ prisa con los preparativos.

4. "¡Qué suerte _____ nosotros!" exclama el señor Johnson.

5. "Es importante _____ cuidado", insiste la señora Johnson.

La navaja

"Tienes razón, Pedro. Los jaguares son muy peligrosos, y es necesario tener mucho cuidado. Al llegar°* a México, vamos a comprar una navaja grande porque no se permite° transportar objetos
5 metálicos en el avión".

"¿Por qué no, Papá?" pregunta Pedro.

Al llegar: *On arriving*

no se permite: *it is not permitted*

---

* **al** plus the verb infinitive = *on/upon* plus verb + *ing*
(e.g., **al llegar** = *on/upon arriving*; **al ver** = *on seeing*)

"Porque hay terroristas en nuestro° mundo que llevan° armas para secuestrar° los aviones. Ellos son tan peligrosos como° los jaguares en el mundo de los
10 mayas", contesta el señor Johnson.

"¡Qué barbaridad!"° exclama Pedro. "Prefiero los jaguares!"

nuestro: *our*

llevan: *carry*
secuestrar: *hijack*
tan . . . como: *as . . . as*

¡Qué barbaridad!: *How awful!*

Actividades

A. Preguntas. Answer these questions either orally or in writing .

1. ¿Por qué es necesario tener cuidado con los jaguares?
2. ¿Qué van a comprar los Johnson en México?
3. ¿Por qué llevan armas los terroristas?
4. En el mundo de los mayas, ¿cómo son los jaguares?
5. ¿Qué prefiere Pedro, los terroristas o los animales feroces?

B. Empareja. Draw a line to match each Spanish sentence in Column A with its English meaning in Column B.

A	B
1. Tengo trece años.	a. She is always hungry.
2. ¿Quiénes tienen razón?	b. Why are you in a hurry?
3. Tenemos mucho calor.	c. I am thirteen years old.
4. ¿Por qué tienes prisa?	d. Who are right?
5. Ella siempre tiene hambre.	e. We are very hot.

C. ¿Sí o no? Write **sí** if the sentence is true according to the story. If the sentence is false, write **no;** then rewrite the sentence by correcting the underlined words.

1. Es necesario tener mucho <u>sueño</u> en la selva.

_____

2. <u>Se permite</u> transportar objetos metálicos en el avión.

_____

3. Los terroristas llevan <u>maletas</u> para secuestrar los aviones.

_____

4. Al llegar a México, los Johnson van a comprar una <u>cámara</u>.

_____

5. Pedro prefiere los <u>jaguares</u> a los terroristas.

_____

D. ¿Cómo se dice? *(How do you say?)* Complete the sentences by translating the words in brackets into Spanish.

1. Pedro busca una navaja porque _____ de los
[he is afraid]

jaguares.

2. Los Johnson van a _____ al llegar a México.
[to be very careful]

3. "_____, Mamá", gritan Catalina y Pedro.
[We are right]

4. Los terroristas _____ porque van a secuestrar
[are in a hurry]

el avión.

5. "¡Tú _____, Pedro!" exclama Catalina.
[are lucky]

E. ¡Dibujemos! Known as "the killer that overcame its prey in a single bound," the jaguar was both feared and worshiped by the Mayas.
    Was the jaguar the god of the underworld, with strange, magical powers? Or was he the sun god, traveling underground during the night and causing volcanoes to explode in violence over a sleeping, green jungle?

LOOK DEEPLY INTO THE JAGUAR'S MOUTH
AND IMAGINE . . .

cueva *(cave)*, **fuego** *(fire)*, **volcán** *(volcano)*, **sol** *(sun)*.

Then, on a separate sheet of paper, draw this mystical jaguar "con sus garras fuertes, sus ojos siniestros y sus dientes enormes."

Could the sun god have been born in a volcano?

FREE YOUR IMAGINATION!

"Viajo durante la noche
en forma de explosiones volcánicas.
Hay una conexión
entre cueva, fuego, volcán y sol.
Soy un dios ATERRADOR!
¿Quién soy?"

Prowling jaguar from mural at Na-Bolom, San Cristóbal de Las Casas

Estar preparados

5

Antes de leer

Adjectives

Adjectives describe nouns. Spanish adjectives must agree in gender (masculine or feminine) and number (singular or plural) with the nouns they describe. Most adjectives end in **-o, -os** (masculine) and **-a, -as** (feminine). Recognizing adjectives and being able to match them to the nouns they modify will help you become a better reader.

Add the appropriate ending to each adjective in these sentences.

1. Catalina y Pedro no son mexican_____. Son american_____.

2. Catalina es una chica muy aventurer_____. Pedro también es

   aventurer_____.

3. La familia Johnson desea ver las aves exótic_____, y las selvas

   misterios_____ de México. ¿Desean ver también los murciélagos

   negr_____?

Estar preparados

"Mamá, ¿dónde está la linterna?"° pregunta Catalina. "Necesitamos también el botiquín para nuestras heriditas".°

"¡Qué buena idea!" exclama la señora
5 Johnson. "Aquí están. Aunque° no tengo miedo de los animales salvajes ni° de los insectos carnívoros, ESTAR PREPARADA es mi lema".°

"¡Ay, Mamá! Con la navaja de Pedro y una
10 sartén° de hierro,° tenemos armas contra los animales más horrorosos de la selva".

linterna: *flashlight*

heriditas: *cuts and bruises*

Aunque: *Although*

ni: *nor*

lema: *motto*

sartén: *frying pan* • hierro: *iron*

"¿Una sartén de hierro?" pregunta la señora Johnson.

"Sí. ¡Para golpear° a los animales feroces
15 en la cabeza!"°

Aunque las dos se ríen,° imaginan la primera noche oscura en la selva, con los gritos° salvajes de los animales y las aves, y un millón de ojos escondidos° que las miran
20 fijamente.°

"Protección . . . ¡Ojalá!"° murmura la señora Johnson.

Para golpear: *To hit*

cabeza: *head*

se ríen: *laugh*

gritos: *screams*

escondidos: *hidden* • miran fijamente: *stare*

¡Ojalá!: *Hopefully!*

Actividades

A. Preguntas. Answer these questions either orally or in writing on a separate sheet of paper.

1. ¿Qué busca Catalina?
2. ¿Tiene miedo la señora Johnson de los animales y de los insectos de la selva?
3. ¿De quién es el lema ESTAR PREPARADA?
4. ¿Qué va a hacer Catalina con la sartén?
5. ¿Qué imaginan Catalina y la señora Johnson?

B. ¿a, b o c? Circle the correct answer.

1. **Botiquín** (line 2) probably means
   a. knife.
   b. first-aid kit.
   c. boat.

2. **Oscura** (line 17) probably means
   a. quiet.
   b. scary.
   c. dark.

3. **Murmura** (line 21) probably means
   a. shouts.
   b. cries.
   c. whispers.

C. En orden. Arrange the words to form correct sentences. Be sure to punctuate and capitalize!

1. linterna / está / dónde / la

   _____

2. buena / qué / idea

   _____

3. feroces / golpear / cabeza / en / los animales / la / a / para

_____

4. noche / imaginan / la / oscura / primera

_____

5. lema / estar / mi / es / preparada

_____

¿Sabes?

The word **ojalá** is of Arabic origin, as are many common words in both English and Spanish. **Ojalá** originally was a cry to Allah, the God of Islam, for help or hope. Picture thousands of Moslems, kneeling low on a temple floor and crying out in anguish to Allah for help.

> "Oh Allah . . . Oh . . . Al . . . lah"
> . . . O . . . ja . . . la   . . . Ojalá

"¡Ojalá!" murmura la señora Johnson. (She needs help too!)

In the seventh century A.D., Mohammed founded a new religion in the Middle East called Islam. It spread rapidly throughout the Arabian lands, into Persia, Egypt, and North Africa. Then in the early eighth century, the Moors, an Arabic tribe from North Africa, invaded Spain and remained in control for almost 800 years! Because of that Moorish occupation, many Arabic words became part of the Spanish, English, Italian, and French languages.

English	Arabic	Spanish
orange	naranj	naranja
cotton	alqutn	algodón
sugar	sukkar	azúcar

CAPÍTULO

Un campamento

6

Antes de leer

Ser and estar

There are two verbs in Spanish that have the English meaning *to be*: **ser** and **estar**. But these verbs each have a different use.

ser tells:	**estar** tells:
who you are	how you feel
what you are like	what your mood is
where you are from	temporary state or condition
your profession	location or position
your nationality	
what things are made of	
time	

Ser and **estar** are irregular verbs. They are conjugated as follows:

yo	soy	yo	estoy
tú	eres	tú	estás
él		él	
ella }	es	ella }	está
usted		usted	
nosotros, -as	somos	nosotros, -as	estamos
(vosotros, -as	sois)	(vosotros, -as	estáis)
ellos		ellos	
ellas }	son	ellas }	están
ustedes		ustedes	

Fill in the blanks with the correct forms of **ser** *and* **estar**.

1. Los Johnson _____ aventureros.

2. Catalina _____ valiente y Pedro _____ intrépido.

3. Nosotros _____ de México.

4. La sartén _____ de hierro.

5. _____ las tres de la tarde.

1. Yo _____ contento.

2. El jaguar _____ en la selva.

3. Ellos _____ enfermos.

4. ¿Dónde _____ tú?

5. La comida _____ fría.

Un campamento

"Aquí está la lista del equipo° para acampar. Uno de nuestros campamentos está en la profundidad de la selva tropical, en un valle encerrado° por la selva. Estamos cerca de° Palenque, una de las ruinas más
5 famosas de los mayas", revela el señor Johnson.

equipo: *equipment*

encerrado: *enclosed*

cerca de: *near*

"¿Hay tumbas y esqueletos en las pirámides?" pregunta Pedro con entusiasmo.

"Sí. En Palenque hay una escalera° secreta al fondo° de la pirámide, y una tumba misteriosa . . ."
10 "Perdóname, Papá. ¡Estamos listos! Es muy tarde. ¡Tenemos que salir° o vamos a perder el avión!" grita Catalina.

escalera: *stairway*

fondo: *bottom*

Tenemos que salir: *We have to leave*

"¡Olé! ¡Vámonos° al aeropuerto!" exclaman todos.

¡Vámonos!: *Let's go!*

Actividades

A. Preguntas. Answer these questions either orally or in writing on a separate sheet of paper.

1. ¿De qué es la lista de los Johnson?
2. ¿Dónde va a estar un campamento de los Johnson?
3. ¿Qué es Palenque?
4. ¿Qué hay al fondo de la pirámide?
5. ¿Por qué tienen que salir los Johnson?

B. ¿a, b o c? Circle the correct answer.

1. In line 1, **lista** probably means
   a. listen.
   b. list.
   c. ready.

2. **Profundidad** (line 2) probably means
   a. profound.
   b. depths.
   c. height.

3. **Un valle** (line 3) is
   a. a mountain top.
   b. a valley.
   c. a desert.

4. In line 10, **listos** probably means
   a. listless.
   b. lists.
   c. ready.

5. In line 11, **perder** probably means
   a. to lose.
   b. to miss.
   c. to find.

C. Crucigrama. Fill in the crossword puzzle with the correct form of **ser** or **estar**.

Across

1. La tarántula _____ en la hamaca.

Down

1. Yo _____ alegre.

2. ¡_____ un esqueleto!

Across	Down

2. Catalina _____ una

exploradora.

3. Nosotros _____

entusiasmados.

5. Yo _____ maya.

7. Tú _____ aventurero,

¿no?

4. Nosotros _____

indios.

5. Las aves _____

exóticas.

6. _____ significa *to be*.

D. Categorías. Read the Johnson's list. Then put the camping
equipment under the correct categories.

la lista del equipo

dos tiendas de campaña *(two tents)*
cuatro sacos para dormir *(four sleeping bags)*
un hornillo *(portable stove)*
un tanque para gas butano
unas sartenes
utensilios de cocina *(kitchen utensils)*

dos linternas
el botiquín
cuatro hamacas
una navaja
los fósforos *(matches)*
las velas *(candles)*

para comer	para dormir	para protección
_____	_____	_____
_____	_____	_____
_____	_____	_____
_____	_____	_____
_____	_____	_____

Palenque, Temple of the Inscriptions.
Pacal's tomb is at the bottom of the
secret stairway in the heart of the
pyramid.

El aeropuerto

7

Antes de leer

Thinking Ahead

Airports are jumping-off places into new worlds, new challenges. There is always excitement, tension, and an air of expectation at an airport.

Passengers on national, or domestic, flights will explore the wonders of the United States, while passengers on international flights will venture beyond the boundaries of this country to visit other parts of the world. They will experience new cultures, languages, and architecture, as well as different foods and musical sounds.

Imagine that you have just been given a ticket to Tierra del Fuego. If you don't know where it is, or which hemisphere it is in, rush to your atlas or encyclopedia to research the area. What is the climate? Is it an undeveloped area? Does it have an interesting history or name?

Armed with this information, circle the things that you will need before you can board the plane.

    a. un hornillo   **f.** un diccionario

    b. el pasaporte   **g.** una tarjeta de turista *(tourist card)*

    c. inyecciones   **h.** maletas

    d. una sartén de hierro   **i.** binoculares

    e. pasajes *(tickets)*   **j.** un suéter

El aeropuerto

La familia Johnson está muy alegre.°
Llegan al aeropuerto con las maletas, el
equipo para acampar, los pasaportes, las
tarjetas de turista, los pasajes y unos libros
5 sobre los mayas para leer durante el vuelo.°

"¡Qué gentío!"° exclama la señora Johnson
al ver a la multitud de viajeros.

"El aeropuerto es un mini-mundo, una
miniatura del mundo entero. Miren, hay

alegre: *cheerful*

vuelo: *flight*

gentío: *crowd*

10 personas de diferentes razas,° diferentes

    aspectos° y de todas las edades.° Hay gordos,

    flacos, tristes° y contentos. Hay reuniones y

    despedidas",° nota el señor Johnson.

       De repente anuncia un altavoz:° "El vuelo

15 número 236 con destino a México está listo.

    Por favor, abordar".

       "¡Arriba, arriba!"° gritan Catalina y Pedro,

    y todos suben° al avión.

razas: races

aspectos: shapes • edades: ages

gordos, flacos, tristes: fat ones, thin ones, sad ones
despedidas: goodbyes

altavoz: loudspeaker

¡Arriba!: Come on!

suben: get on

Actividades

A. Preguntas. Answer these questions either orally or in writing on a separate sheet of paper.

1. ¿Por qué está alegre la familia Johnson?
2. ¿Qué llevan al aeropuerto?
3. Según el señor Johnson, ¿cómo es el aeropuerto?
4. ¿Adónde va el vuelo número 236?
5. ¿Quiénes suben al avión?

B. Cuál no va? Cross out the word that does not belong in each group.

1. las maletas	los flacos	el equipo	los libros mayas
2. los viajeros	el piloto	los Johnson	las edades
3. un mini-mundo	la multitud	de repente	los pasajeros
4. las tarjetas de turista	los pasajes	los gordos	los pasaportes

C. Empareja. Draw a line to match each Spanish phrase in Column A with its English meaning in Column B.

A	B
1. reuniones y despedidas	a. suddenly
2. de repente	b. they get on the plane
3. llegan con las maletas	c. the whole world
4. suben al avión	d. they arrive with suitcases
5. el mundo entero	e. reunions and goodbyes

D. ¿Y tú? Answer these questions in complete sentences.

1. ¿Cuántos años tienes?
2. ¿Eres gordo(a) o flaco(a)?
3. ¿Eres alto(a) or bajo(a)?
4. ¿Tienes hermanos(as)?
5. ¿Cuántas personas hay en tu familia?

6. ¿Estás triste o contento(a) hoy?

7. ¿Adónde viaja tu familia en verano?

8. ¿Deseas hacer un viaje como el de los Johnson?

¿Sabes?

When you plan your week's schedule, are you aware that the name of each day means something special? In Spanish, most come from Roman mythology.

lunes (Monday)	el día dedicado a la luna *(moon)*
martes (Tuesday)	dedicado a Marte, dios *(god)* de la guerra *(war)*
miércoles (Wednesday)	dedicado a Mercurio, el mensajero *(messenger)* de los dioses
jueves (Thursday)	en honor de Júpiter *(Jove)*, rey *(king)* de los dioses
viernes (Friday)	en honor de Venus, la diosa *(goddess)* del amor *(love)*
sábado (Saturday)	de *shabbāth* (Hebrew for Sabbath)
domingo (Sunday)	dedicado a Dominus, el Señor *(the Lord)*

Chiapas Indians. The number and color of the ribbons on their hats have special meanings.

En el avión

8

Antes de leer

¡Exclamaciones!

On safari, you will find yourself in many strange situations. Draw a line to match each exclamation in Column A with its meaning in Column B.

A	B
1. ¡Qué peligroso!	**a.** How awful!
2. ¡Qué gentío!	**b.** All aboard!
3. ¡Olé!	**c.** Let's go!
4. ¡Por favor, abordar!	**d.** You don't say!
5. ¡Ojalá!	**e.** How dangerous!
6. ¡Qué barbaridad!	**f.** Bravo!
7. ¡Vámonos!	**g.** What a crowd!
8. ¡No me digas!	**h.** Here's hoping!

¡OJO! A Spanish exclamation begins with an upside-down exclamation mark (¡) and ends with a regular exclamation mark (!). **Qué** always has an accent mark (ʹ) when it introduces an exclamation.

En el avión

"Abróchense los cinturones,° por favor",
anuncia la azafata.° "En caso de emergencia,
hay chalecos salvavidas° debajo de° sus
asientos".

5 Los Johnson leen tranquilamente sus
libros sobre los mayas y practican español.
Por la ventanilla, Catalina y Pedro miran el
paisaje.°

 "Imagínate, Catalina. Vamos a un mundo
10 oculto por la selva. Hay pirámides, tumbas y

Abróchense los cinturones: *Fasten your seatbelts*
azafata: *stewardess*

chalecos salvavidas: *life jackets*
debajo de: *under*

paisaje: *landscape*

momias desconocidas° en las colinas.° Todo
está cubierto° por una densa vegetación".

"¡Es fascinante!" exclama Catalina,
mirando el mundo misterioso. "Los
15 arqueólogos son los que descubren° las
civilizaciones perdidas° y resucitan° la vida de
épocas muertas",° continúa ella.

desconocidas: *unknown* • colinas: *hills*

cubierto: *covered*

descubren: *discover*

perdidas: *lost*
resucitan – resurrect
muertas: *dead*

Actividades

A. Preguntas. Answer these questions either orally or in writing on a separate sheet of paper.

1. ¿Qué anuncia la azafata?
2. ¿Dónde están los chalecos salvavidas?
3. ¿Qué leen los Johnson?
4. Según Catalina, ¿qué hacen los arqueólogos?

B. ¿a, b o c? Circle the correct answer.

1. Los cinturones sirven para
   a. comida.
   b. protección.
   c. el paisaje.

2. Debajo de los asientos hay
   a. unos libros sobre los mayas.
   b. un mundo escondido.
   c. chalecos salvavidas.

3. Cubiertas por la vegetación hay
   a. civilizaciones perdidas.
   b. montañas altas.
   c. arqueólogos.

4. Según Catalina, la vida de los arqueólogos es fascinante porque
   a. son españoles.
   b. miran por la ventanilla.
   c. exploran mundos antiguos.

C. ¡Exclamaciones! En cada situación, ¿qué gritas tú? From the list on page 41, choose an appropriate exclamation for each of the following situations:

1. Dos terroristas entran en la cabina y gritan, "¡Es un secuestro!"
2. Tú notas que el piloto duerme.
3. Hay solamente un chaleco salvavidas en el avión.
4. Un arqueólogo descubre un gran tesoro en una cueva.

D. ¡Dibujemos! On a separate sheet of paper, draw an exciting, unusual, or dramatic situation from your own imagination and label it with an appropriate exclamation.

El vuelo continúa

9

Antes de leer

Word Families

Knowledge of word families gives you clues to understanding a foreign language. The root of the word will identify the family, and from there you will be able to figure out the variations of that root.

The Spanish word **escribir** means *to write*, and is very similar to its Latin root *scribere*. Does it remind you of *scribble, scribe,* or *script*? Of course! In Spanish, some members of the same family are **escritorio** *(desk)*, **escrito** *(written)*, **escritor,-ra** *(writer)*, and **escritura** *(writing)*.

What is the common denominator of this family of words?

When you spot any variation of **escri,** you will probably be able to guess its meaning from the context.

El vuelo continúa

Catalina y Pedro continúan su conversación con voces animadas.

"¡Pedro! Si podemos encontrar° una pista°—una estatua con jeroglíficos o una piedra clave° para
5 descifrar la escritura—¡vamos a tener una llave° a los secretos de los mayas!"

encontrar: *find* • pista: *clue* • piedra clave: *keystone*

llave: *key*

"¡Sí, Catalina! ¡Imagínate el impacto de nuestro descubrimiento! Puede cambiar° la historia de los mayas y de su desaparición".

cambiar: *change*

10 "¡Ay, Pedro! ¡Vamos a ser famosos! ¡Qué orgullosos° van a estar nuestros padres!"

orgullosos: *proud*

"¡Y qué envidia van a sentir° los arqueólogos!"
exclama Pedro, con una sonrisa° grande.

sentir: *feel*

sonrisa: *smile*

"¡Pasajeros! Llegamos a México. Abróchense los
15 cinturones, por favor", interrumpe la voz segura del
piloto.

Con expresiones extáticas, Catalina y Pedro dan
abrazos fuertes a sus padres.

Todos bajan del avión y entran en el mundo de los
20 mayas.

Actividades

A. Preguntas. Answer these questions ~~either orally or~~ on a separate ~~sheet of pap~~er.

1. ¿Cómo es la conversación de Catalina y Pedro?
2. ¿Qué desean encontrar Catalina y Pedro en la selva de México?
3. ¿Quiénes van a ser famosos? ¿Por qué?
4. ¿Qué van a sentir los arqueólogos? ¿Por qué?
5. Al bajar del avión, ¿cómo están los Johnson?

B. ¿a, b o c? Circle the correct answer.

1. If **descubrir** means *to discover*, **descubrimiento** (line 8) probably means
   a. cover-up.
   b. discovery.
   c. uncovering.

2. If **parecer** means *to appear or seem to be*, **desaparición** (line 9) probably means
   a. disappearance.
   b. despair.
   c. dislike.

3. The noun **brazos** means *arms*, so **abrazos** (line 18) are probably
   a. kisses.
   b. hugs.
   c. winks.

C. Frases completas. Create an original sentence with each of the following words or phrases.

1. emergencia
2. paisaje
3. densa vegetación
4. civilizaciones perdidas
5. los arqueólogos

D.

aterrizar   territorio

What do these words have in common? *Terra* is the Latin
word for *earth* or *land*, and **tierra** means the same in Spanish.
Many Latin, English, Spanish, and French words with that
root have something to do with the earth.

Para completar. Read the following sentences carefully. Then choose
the word that best completes each sentence, and write it in the space.

terremoto	territorio	aterrizar	terraza	extraterrestre

1. Al llegar a México, el avión va a _____.

2. La _____ está llena de flores exóticas.

3. El _____ de los mayas es la península de Yucatán.

4. Un ser del espacio exterior es un _____.

5. Cuando la tierra tiembla, ¡es un _____!

¿Sabes?

Another means of communication is "body language," that is, the way
we walk, talk, enter a room, meet people, and so on. In every culture
body language conveys as much meaning as words. Actors, when
learning a new part, must also learn how to move like people of all
ages. Before soundtracks were added to the movies, body language was
the only way a story could be understood.

There are different ways to greet people or say goodbye. Frenchmen
kiss each other on both cheeks. Laplanders rub noses, and Japanese
bow to each other. A Chinaman in olden times shook his own hand.
Soldiers salute, while Englishmen and Americans shake hands.

Baseball catchers, orchestra conductors, and police officers all have their own set of signals that, without words, convey definite messages.

1. In front of the class, see if you can walk like:
   - an old man
   - a five-year-old
   - a teenager

2. Let your classmates guess! Make several gestures that convey:
   - excitement (your favorite team is about to score)
   - fear (you are at a scary movie)
   - anger (a car splashes mud on your new clothes)

(Cover your face if you want to, so that your facial expression won't give you away!)

Stelae or carved monolith. Archaeologists are making great progress in deciphering Mayan hieroglyphics.

CAPÍTULO

La llegada

10

Antes de leer

Verb Endings

In Spanish, the ending of a verb gives a clue as to the verb's subject (the doer of the action). Subject pronouns (**yo, tú, él, ella, usted [Ud.], nosotros,-as, ellos,-as, ustedes [Uds.]**) are often not used. Since the verb form for the third person singular (**él, ella, Ud.**) is identical, as is the third person plural form (**ellos,-as** and **Uds.**), you must figure out the verb's subject from the context of the sentence.

Guess what pronouns are missing in each of these sentences.

1. _____ estoy muy bien. ¿Cómo estás _____?

2. Catalina no está aquí hoy. _____ está en el aeropuerto.

3. Los Johnson no son estudiantes. _____ son profesores.

La llegada

¡Qué gentío! ¡Qué confusión! ¡El aeropuerto
internacional de la Ciudad de México es un MAXI-
mundo!

"¡Bienvenidos a México!" grita un maletero.°   maletero: *porter*
5 "¿Desean un taxi?"

"Sí, deseamos un taxi, por favor. Tenemos
reservaciones en un hotel en la ciudad", responde
Pedro, orgulloso del buen español que habla.

El maletero hace señales con la mano y de repente
10 llega un taxi.

"Gracias, señor", dice Catalina. "Es muy amable".

"Ustedes hablan español como mexicanos", comenta el muchacho con admiración.

"Tengo miedo de hablar español enfrente de
15 Catalina y Pedro", murmura el señor Johnson a su esposa. "¡Hablan muy, muy bien!"

Los Johnson suben al taxi con sus maletas y salen° salen: *leave*
para la ciudad más poblada° del mundo. más poblada: *most populated*

Actividades

A. Preguntas. Answer these questions either orally or in writing on a separate sheet of paper.

1. ¿Cómo es el aeropuerto de la Ciudad de México?
2. ¿Qué hace un maletero?
3. ¿Quiénes hablan español como mexicanos?
4. ¿Por qué tiene miedo de hablar español el señor Johnson?
5. ¿Cómo se llama la ciudad más poblada del mundo?

B. ¿a, b o c? Circle the correct answer.

1. **¡Bienvenidos a México!** (line 4) probably means
   a. You have arrived in Mexico!
   b. Welcome to Mexico!
   c. Have a good time in Mexico!

2. **Hace señales** (line 9) probably means
   a. claps.
   b. whistles.
   c. signals.

3. **Dice** (line 11) probably means
   a. answers.
   b. talks.
   c. says.

4. **Enfrente de** (line 14) probably means
   a. in front of.
   b. next to.
   c. instead of.

5. **Esposa** (line 16) probably means
   a. sister.
   b. daughter.
   c. wife.

C. Frases completas. Create an original sentence with each of the following words or phrases.

1. el maletero
2. orgulloso
3. hace señales

4. tengo miedo
5. de repente

D. Para completar. Add the appropriate subject pronoun to each of these sentences. Refer to the reading to find out the probable subject for each verb.

1. ¿Desean _____ un taxi?

2. Sí, _____ deseamos un taxi.

3. _____ es muy amable.

4. _____ hablan español como mexicanos.

5. _____ tengo miedo de hablar español.

E. ¡Dibujemos! On a separate sheet of paper, draw the airport. Show people of all shapes, sizes, ages, and expressions. There are reunions and goodbyes, laughter and tears, tension and excitement.

Mexico City's international airport

CAPÍTULO

La ciudad

11

Antes de leer

Adjectives

Many Spanish adjectives can come either before or after the noun. Adjectives follow the noun to emphasize a special characteristic (color, shape, nationality, religion) or to differentiate the noun from other members of its group (**arte maya**).

Translate these phrases into Spanish. Keep in mind the position of the adjectives and their gender and number agreement.

1. a dangerous knife _____

2. an amiable porter _____

3. two white taxis _____

4. ecstatic expressions _____

La ciudad

Toda la familia mira la ciudad fabulosa por
las ventanillas del taxi. Hay contrastes
enormes. Viajan por calles lujosas° donde hay   lujosas: *luxurious*
casas que parecen palacios, con estatuas
5 espléndidas y fuentes° elegantes. Los Johnson   fuentes: *fountains*
también ven calles pequeñas. En estas calles
hay casitas de adobe con patios llenos de
niños, perros, cabras, gallinas y cerdos.°   cabras, gallinas y cerdos: *goats, hens, and pigs*

    "¡Mira, Pedro!" exclama Catalina,
10 encantada. "Hay arquitectura moderna y

edificios muy antiguos. Los rascacielos° tocan las nubes.° También hay parques tropicales llenos de flores bonitas y árboles magníficos".

"Cada país° del mundo tiene su identidad
15 especial, sus propios° colores, sonidos, sabores y olores",° comenta el señor Johnson.

"Es verdad. Y México estimula todos los sentidos° a la vez: la vista, el oído, el olfato, el gusto y el tacto",° dice la señora Johnson.

rascacielos: *skyscrapers*

nubes: *clouds*

país: *country*

propios: *own* • sonidos, sabores y olores: *sounds, flavors, and smells*

sentidos: *senses* • vista, oído, olfato, gusto y tacto: *sight, hearing, smell, taste, and touch*

Actividades

A. Preguntas. Answer these questions either orally or in writing on a separate sheet of paper.

1. ¿Qué impresión tiene la familia Johnson de la capital mexicana?
2. ¿Qué contrastes hay en la ciudad?
3. ¿Qué hay en las calles pequeñas?
4. ¿Qué tiene de especial cada país del mundo?
5. ¿Qué sentidos estimula México? ¿Puedes mencionar un ejemplo para cada sentido?

B. Categorías. Cross out the word that does not belong in each category.

1. estatuas	fuentes	parques	niños
2. colores	calles	sonidos	sabores
3. cerdos	taxis	maleteros	maletas
4. olfato	vista	moderno	tacto
5. cabras	edificios	gallinas	perros

C. Combinaciones. Draw a line from each noun to the adjective it can be used with. Match the nouns and adjectives according to their meaning, gender, and number. Then on a separate sheet of paper, write a sentence for each combination.

1. cerdo	a. blancas
2. nubes	b. lujoso
3. parques	c. antigua
4. palacio	d. gordo
5. ciudad	e. tropicales

¿Sabes?

Spanish compound nouns are lots of fun. They are formed by fusing a verb root with a noun to create a new word. You already know two compound nouns: **rascacielos** and **salvavidas**. Let's learn some more!

el abrelatas	can opener	**abrir**	to open
		latas	cans
el tocadiscos	record player	**tocar**	to play (music)
		discos	records
el guardarropa	wardrobe,	**guardar**	to guard,
	closet		to save
		ropa	clothes
el lavaplatos	dishwasher	**lavar**	to wash
		platos	plates
el guardapolvo	apron, smock	**guardar**	to guard
		polvo	dust
el limpiaparabrisas	windshield	**limpiar**	to clean
	wiper	**parar**	to stop
		brisas	wind
el picaflor	hummingbird	**picar**	to sting,
			to puncture
		flor	flower
el sacacorchos	corkscrew	**sacar**	to pull out
		corchos	corks

Review your verb list and try to guess what these compound nouns mean.

1. el limpiachimeneas
2. el limpiabotas

3. el lavamanos
4. el guardacostas

Escoge. Choose five of the compound nouns above ~~and draw a picture of them~~. Then write a sentence or two in Spanish about each ~~of your drawings. Be ready to show and explain your work to the class~~.

Old Spanish hacienda

CAPÍTULO

Más impresiones

12

Antes de leer

Related Words

You can usually guess the meaning of an unfamiliar word if it is related to another word that you already know.

Look at these sentences and try to figure out the meaning of the underlined words.

1. El avión <u>vuela</u> a una <u>altura</u> de 9,760 metros.
2. Una <u>bienvenida</u> típica en los países hispanos es "Mi casa es tu casa".
3. La <u>comida</u> mexicana es <u>sabrosa</u>.

What familiar Spanish words helped you understand the sentences? Write them here.

1. vuela _____ altura _____

2. bienvenida _____

3. comida _____ sabrosa _____

Más impresiones

Con la cabeza casi fuera° de la ventanilla, Pedro grita, "¡Los sonidos de México! ¡Escucha, Catalina! ¡La música alegre, los gritos fuertes, los cláxones,° las campanas,° 5 los camiones,° los gallos,° los perros y los rebuznos° de los burros! ¡Increíble! ¡Qué alegría!"

"¡Qué tráfico!" protesta el taxista. "Y el tráfico crea demasiada contaminación.° Como

casi fuera: *almost out*

cláxones: *horns* • campanas: *bells*
camiones: *trucks* • gallos: *roosters*
rebuznos: *braying*

contaminación: *pollution*

10 la ciudad tiene más de 18 millones de
personas y el valle está rodeado° de   rodeado: *surrounded*
montañas, la contaminación está atrapada en
el valle".
  "En nuestro país también tenemos mucha
15 contaminación", comenta Catalina con
tristeza. "Los animales, los peces,° las aves y   peces: *fish*
los insectos sufren como nosotros. ¡Todos
somos víctimas!"

Actividades

A. Preguntas. Answer these questions either orally or in writing on a separate sheet of paper.

1. ¿Cuáles son los sonidos de la Ciudad de México?
2. ¿Por qué hay tanta contaminación en la capital mexicana?
3. Según Catalina, ¿quiénes son las víctimas de la contaminación?
4. ¿Cuántas personas viven en la Ciudad de México?
5. En tu opinión, ¿cuál es la solución al problema de la contaminación?

B. ¿Cómo se dice? Translate these sentences into English.

1. La cabeza de Pedro está casi fuera de la ventanilla.

   _____

2. En las calles de la ciudad, escuchamos cláxones, campanas, gallos, perros y burros.

   _____

3. El valle está rodeado de montañas altas.

   _____

4. La gente, los animales y los peces sufren por la contaminación.

   _____

C. Para completar.

1. If **gritar** means *to shout,* **gritos** (line 4) are probably

   _____.

2. If **alegre** means *happy,* **alegría** (line 7) probably means

   _____.

3. Taxista (line 8) must mean _____.

4. If **triste** means *sad,* **tristeza** (line 16) probably means

_____.

D. Juego de categorías: Los cinco sentidos. On a separate sheet of paper, draw the part of the body that represents each of the five senses.

Ejemplo: Dibuja un para **la vista**.

una _____ para **el oído**.

un(a) _____ para **el tacto**.

una _____ para **el olfato**.

una _____ para **gusto**.

Read the following list carefully and draw the symbol that you associate with each of these phrases. Some phrases might excite more than one of our five senses!

1. las campanas

2. las flores tropicales

3. la contaminación

4. los gallos, cerdos y burros

5. fuentes elegantes

6. la comida

7. los cláxones

8. la arquitectura

9. los patios llenos de niños

10. la música alegre

Typical Mayan house with thatched roof

CAPÍTULO

El hotel

13

Antes de leer

Adjectives and Adverbs

Word order in English and Spanish sentences is similar. (One exception: descriptive adjectives usually *follow* the noun.)

It is usually easy to figure out the part of speech of individual words, as there are valuable clues that you can use to identify certain types of words. Many adverbs, for example, end in *-ly* in English *(slowly, completely)* and in **-mente** in Spanish (**lentamente, completamente**). These adverbs are formed by adding **-mente** to the feminine form of the adjective.

¡OJO! Remember that not all feminine adjectives end in **-a**. Adjectives that end in **-e** or a consonant (**enorme, final**) use the same form to describe both masculine and feminine nouns. Such adjectives have only two forms, singular and plural.

What do you think these adverbs mean? Write the adjectives they are formed from.

1. enormemente _____

2. orgullosamente _____

3. especialmente _____

El hotel

"¡Aquí está el hotel, señores", dice el
taxista al parar enfrente de un edificio
colonial decorado con flores exóticas.

Los Johnson salen rápidamente del taxi y
5 sacan el equipaje° del baúl.° Después, el   equipaje: *baggage* • baúl: *trunk*
señor Johnson paga al taxista con pesos
mexicanos.

"¡Vayan con Dios!" exclama el taxista con
una sonrisa.

"Gracias, señor. Es muy amable", responde
10 la señora Johnson. Ella repite la frase de
Catalina porque también desea parecer
mexicana.

La familia entra en el vestíbulo del hotel.
¡Qué bonito es! En el centro hay una fuente

¹⁵ llena de gardenias flotantes. Un loro° gordo,   loro: *parrot*
con plumas largas, grita ruidosamente° en su   ruidosamente: *noisily*
jaula.°   jaula: *cage*

    "Bienvenidos, señor y señora Johnson",
saluda° el recepcionista. "Y ustedes también,   saluda: *greets*
²⁰ jóvenes".

    "¡Hola, amigos!" grita el loro, que salta°   salta: *jumps*
alegremente en su jaula.

    "Ustedes deben descansar° inmediatamente   descansar: *rest*
para acostumbrarse a la altura, que es más
²⁵ de 2,000 metros", recomienda el
recepcionista.

    "¡Qué buena idea!" dice la señora Johnson,
haciendo esfuerzos° para respirar.   haciendo esfuerzos: *making an effort*

Actividades

A. Sí o no? Write **sí** if the sentence is true according to the story. If the sentence is false, write **no**; then rewrite the sentence correctly.

1. El hotel es un rascacielos moderno.

   _____

2. El señor Johnson paga al taxista con dólares.

   _____

3. El taxista dice "adiós" a los Johnson.

   _____

4. Hay flores exóticas en la jaula.

   _____

5. El recepcionista dice que los Johnson deben caminar mucho para acostumbrarse a la altura de la Ciudad de México.

   _____

6. La capital mexicana está a una altura mayor que la de la capital de los Estados Unidos.

   _____

B. En orden. Number the story events to show their correct order. The first one is done for you.

_____ El loro saluda a los Johnson.

_____ Los Johnson sacan las maletas del taxi.

__1__ El taxista para enfrente del hotel.

_____ El señor Johnson paga al taxista.

_____ El recepcionista saluda a los Johnson.

_____ La señora Johnson habla con el taxista.

C. ¿Cómo se dice? Translate these sentences into Spanish.

1. Where's the luggage?

_____

2. It's in the trunk.

_____

3. The water in the fountain is blue and the gardenias are white.

_____

4. The receptionist greets the Johnsons in the lobby.

_____

5. Do you want to rest?

_____

D. Totalmente en español. Complete this paragraph by changing the adjectives in brackets to adverbs.

El señor Johnson paga _____ al taxista.
[1. generoso]

Entonces, la familia entra _____ en el hotel. El
[2. rápido]

vestíbulo es _____ bonito. Los Johnson van
[3. verdadero]

_____ a la recepción donde el recepcionista los
[4. directo]

saluda _____. Los Johnson comprenden
[5. amable]

_____ al recepcionista porque él habla muy

[6. fácil]

_____ .

[7. claro]

¿Sabes?

Sound is a lively part of almost everyone's world. Each family, each race, each culture has its own set of familiar sounds that are a recognizable means of communication.

Why don't all peoples of the world use the same word for the same sound? A sneeze is a sneeze all over the world. We all sneeze and we all have noses, but here is how a sneeze sounds in different parts of the world.

English: *atchoo*   Russian: *apchi*
Spanish: *atchis*   Chinese: *hah-chee*
French: *atchouin*   Indonesian: *wahing*
German: *hatschi*   Japanese: *gu-gu*

Are Japanese ears shaped differently from French ears? Do people hear sounds differently? Do sneezes come out with an accent in foreign countries?

CAPÍTULO

El primer día

14

Antes de leer

Homonyms

Many Spanish words have more than one English meaning. When you read, it is important to give a word the correct or appropriate meaning, depending on the context of the sentence. For example, **ganar** can mean either *to earn* or *to win*; **tocar** means *to touch, to play* (music, an instrument), or *to sound* (a bell).

Read these sentences and decide the exact meaning of the underlined words.

1. ¿Cuánto <u>gana</u> el señor Johnson?
2. La escuela de Pedro siempre <u>gana</u> el partido *(game)* de béisbol.
3. Catalina <u>toca</u> el piano y canta también.
4. Pedro tiene miedo de <u>tocar</u> al loro.

El primer día

¡Qué despertador° ruidoso, pero tan alegre! Los
sonidos de México dan° la bienvenida a la mañana y
despiertan° a los Johnson. Las campanas, los burros,
los cláxones, los gallos, acompañados de una sinfonía
5 de aves . . . ¡todos a la vez! Es una cacofonía, pero
como es México, parece melódica.
    "No necesito un tanque de oxígeno. Ya° estoy
acostumbrada a la altura", dice Catalina. "Pero sí
necesito comer. ¡Tengo mucha hambre!"
10   "¡Yo también!" grita Pedro.
    "Pues, vamos al Zócalo",° sugiere el señor Johnson.
"Es el corazón de la ciudad. Tenemos que cambiar°
más dólares a pesos mexicanos. En el Zócalo hay

despertador: *alarm clock*
dan: *give*
despiertan: *awaken*

Ya: *Already*

Zócalo: *public square*
cambiar: *exchange*

bancos y restaurantes. También, están el Palacio
15 Nacional, la Catedral y el Museo del Templo Mayor.
Es un verdadero templo azteca, recién° descubierto". **recién:** *recently*

"¡Vámonos!" exclama la señora Johnson. "Quiero° **Quiero:** *I want*
tomar un colectivo* porque son más divertidos y más
baratos° que los taxis. Y así viajamos con los **baratos:** *cheap*
20 mexicanos".

---

* There are expensive cabs and inexpensive cabs in Mexico. A new addition to
public transportation are the **colectivos**, Volkswagen (VW) vans outfitted
with bench seats. They run regular routes, are packed to the ceiling, lots of
fun, and cost about 10% of what a taxi would charge.

Actividades

A. Preguntas. Answer these questions either orally or in writing on a separate sheet of paper.

1. ¿Qué despierta a los Johnson su primer día en la ciudad?
2. ¿Cuáles son los sonidos de México? ¿Cómo son?
3. ¿Por qué no necesita más oxígeno Catalina? ¿Qué necesita?
4. Describe el Zócalo.
5. ¿Cómo son los colectivos? ¿Por qué prefieren los Johnson tomar un colectivo? ¿Hay colectivos en los Estados Unidos?

B. Empareja. Draw a line to match each word in Column A with its synonym in Column B. Then, on a separate sheet of paper, write complete sentences with the words in Column A.

	A		B
1.	cacofonía	a.	centro
2.	sinfonía	b.	recomienda
3.	corazón	c.	ruido
4.	sugiere	d.	dinero
5.	pesos	e.	concierto

C. ¿Cuál es? Look at the story again. Circle the meaning for each word as it is used in this chapter.

1. Mañana (line 2)
   a. tomorrow **b.** morning
2. Todos (line 5)
   a. all of them **b.** everybody
3. Como (line 6)
   a. like **b.** since
4. Peso (line 13)
   a. dollar **b.** weight
5. Que (line 19)
   a. what **b.** than

D. ¡Dibujemos! On a separate sheet of paper, draw a **colectivo** at rush hour in the most populated city in the world.

Desafío: Label the parts of the van in Spanish. Use your dictionary. Be prepared to explain your drawing to the class in Spanish!

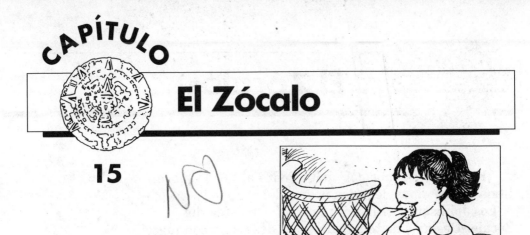

CAPÍTULO 15

El Zócalo

Antes de leer

Research

Even if you have never been to Mexico or to any foreign country, you can imagine what a plaza or main square looks like. If you can't, one solution is to do some research. Reference books such as an encyclopedia, an almanac, a travel book, or an atlas are valuable tools you can use to find out more about subjects you are interested in.

Decide where you would look to find out more information about these Mexican topics.

1. **El Palacio Nacional**: When, why, and by whom was it built?
2. **Los aztecas**: Who were they? Where, when, and how did they live?

El Zócalo

"¡El Zócalo es enorme!" grita Pedro al ver la plaza, llena de personas de todas partes del mundo.

Los Johnson entran en una cafetería cerca del Zócalo. Después de tomar un buen desayuno con jugo, 5 huevos y bolillos° calientes,° salen a la plaza.

bolillos: *rolls* • calientes: *hot*

"¡Qué magníficos son los edificios que rodean la plaza!" exclama Catalina.

La familia entra primero en el Palacio Nacional, el centro de las operaciones de Hernan Cortés en el 10 siglo XVI. Hoy día el presidente mexicano dirige° el gobierno desde el palacio.

dirige: *directs*

"Hay murales de Diego Rivera en las paredes° del patio central", dice Pedro. "Vamos a verlos".

paredes: *walls*

"¡Qué violentos y dramáticos!" exclama Catalina al
15 ver los murales impresionantes.

"Los murales ilustran la historia de México desde
el punto de vista° de los indios y de los
revolucionarios", explica la señora Johnson.

"La Revolución Mexicana es un tiempo de
20 violencia, de huelgas,° y de lucha° contra las
injusticias de un gobierno codicioso.° Pintores
famosos, como Rivera, Orozco y Siquieros, protestan
contra la explotación de los indios y la falta de
derechos° humanos en murales como estos. "Tierra y
25 Libertad" es el tema° de la revolución", continúa el
señor Johnson.

punto de vista: *point of view*

huelgas: *strikes* • lucha: *fight* • codicioso: *greedy*

derechos: *rights*

tema: *theme*

Actividades

A. Preguntas. Answer these questions either orally or in writing on a separate sheet of paper.

1. ¿Qué desayuna la familia Johnson en su primer día en la capital mexicana? ¿Dónde come?
2. ¿Qué comes tú en el desayuno? ¿Dónde desayunas?
3. ¿Por qué es importante el Palacio Nacional?
4. ¿Qué hay en las paredes del patio central del Palacio Nacional? ¿Cómo son?
5. ¿Hay algo similar en este país? ¿Dónde está?
6. ¿Contra qué protestan los muralistas?

B. Vocabulario. Complete these sentences.

1. **Desde** (lines 11 and 16) means _____.

2. **Gobierno** (line 11) means _____.

3. **Murales** (lines 12, 15, and 16) are _____.

4. **Impresionantes** (line 15) means _____.

C. ¿Dónde? The reading in this chapter includes information about some very important people, places, and events in Mexican history. If you wanted to know more about them, where would you look?

1. el Zócalo _____

2. Diego Rivera _____

3. Hernán Cortés _____

4. los revolucionarios _____

5. la independencia de México _____

6. el presidente de México _____

D. En busca de información. Now, choose one of the topics or historical figures from Exercise C, delve into Mexico's exciting past, and report your findings to the class . . . in Spanish!

¿Sabes?

Deep below the Zócalo lies the ancient capital of the Aztec Empire, Tenochtitlán. Known as the Venice of the New World, Tenochtitlán was a city of **chinampas** (floating gardens) with canals, bridges, and long causeways that were connected to the mainland.

Chinampas were "living rafts," made by layers of thick water vegetation cut from the surface and piled up like mats to form a garden plot. Then, mud from the bottom of the canals was spread over these green rafts that were then anchored thoroughly by willow trees planted securely around them. All sorts of crops were raised on these fertile garden plots. Even houses of cane or thatch were built upon these foundations.

This poem is an adaptation of a Nahuatl (Aztec) poem* describing the impressive beauty of this garden paradise.

> The gold-misted city shimmered
> in circles of iridescent color
> like quetzal plumes.†
> Sky-mirrored silver canals undulated among jade islands
> where enshrined chieftains in feathered canopies
> were emplumed in grandeur and power . . .
> An emerald-sweet mist perfumed the sunrise.

Tenochtitlán! The invading Spaniards were amazed by the impressive beauty of this garden paradise.

---

* From *La filosofía nahuatl*, by Miguel León Portillo, Universidad Autónoma de México, México, 1979. This English version is an interpretation by the author.

† The long, green, shimmering tail feathers of the mystical quetzal bird were prized by chieftains and gods. These plumes, used in elaborate headdresses by the high priests, were plucked from the living bird—the god of the air—which was a symbol of freedom.

(If they are lucky, the Johnson family might catch a glimpse of the quetzal bird-god in the cloud forests near the Guatemalan border!)

CAPÍTULO

El corazón de la ciudad

16

Antes de leer

Imperfect Tense

As the Johnson family heads into the jungle to search for the Mayas, they will be entering the past, exploring ancient civilizations. Up until now, only the present tense has been used, but at this point you should be able to recognize and use the past tenses.

The imperfect tense (imperfect because actions have not been completed within a prescribed time in the past) describes what was happening over a period of time. It is used to give the background of an action.

The imperfect also indicates habitual or repeated action in the past: one that happened more than once. It also expresses age, weather, the time of day in the past, and a state of mind with such verbs as **saber** *(to know)*, **querer** *(to want)*, **pensar** *(to think)*, and **creer** *(to believe)*.

To form the imperfect tense of regular **-ar, -er,** and **-ir** verbs, the infinitive ending is dropped and the following endings are added to the stem:

	hablar (-ar)	comer (-er)	vivir (-ir)
yo	habl**aba**	com**ía**	viv**ía**
tú	habl**abas**	com**ías**	viv**ías**
él, ella, usted	habl**aba**	com**ía**	viv**ía**
nosotros, -as	habl**ábamos**	com**íamos**	viv**íamos**
(vosotros, -as	habl**abais**	com**íais**	viv**íais**)
ellos, ellas, ustedes	habl**aban**	com**ían**	viv**ían**

Ser, **ir**, and **ver** are the only irregular verbs in the imperfect tense.

	ser	ir	ver
yo	era	iba	veía
tú	eras	ibas	veías
él, ella, usted	era	iba	veía
nosotros, -as	éramos	íbamos	veíamos
(vosotros, -as	erais	ibais	veíais)
ellos, ellas, ustedes	eran	iban	veían

El corazón de la ciudad

"¿Un secreto sangriento?"° pregunta Pedro
con los ojos brillantes.

    sangriento: *bloody*

"Sí. Debajo del Zócalo, debajo de estos
palacios, iglesias y museos impresionantes
5 habitan los fantasmas° del imperio azteca.
Tenochtitlán era la Venecia del Nuevo
Mundo . . . un paraíso° de canales, puentes,°
pirámides majestuosas y dioses
sanguinarios",° explica el señor Johnson.

    fantasmas: *ghosts*

    paraíso: *paradise* • puentes: *bridges*

    sanguinarios: *bloodthirsty*

10 "¡Qué fantástico!" grita Catalina.

"Los aztecas creían que Huitzilopochtli, el
dios de la guerra, y Tlaloc, el dios de la
lluvia, necesitaban sangre° para ser felices.
Por eso, muchas personas murieron° como
15 ofrendas a los dioses", añade la señora
Johnson.

    sangre: *blood*

    murieron: *died*

"¡Qué horror!" comenta Pedro.

"Según los aztecas, los sacrificios humanos
no eran ni crueles ni horrorosos. Eran
20 absolutamente necesarios para garantizar
una buena vida bajo la protección de los
dioses", explica el señor Johnson.

"¡Increíble!" exclaman Catalina y Pedro, al
imaginar la civilización enterrada° debajo de   enterrada: *buried*
25 sus pies.

"Hoy día, caminamos sobre los esqueletos y
fantasmas del imperio azteca, soldados y
víctimas . . . ¡y millones de corazones sacados
de personas vivas!" grita Pedro con una voz
30 llena de admiración reverente.

Actividades

A. Preguntas. Answer these questions either orally or in writing on a separate sheet of paper.

1. ¿Cuál es el secreto del Zócalo?
2. ¿Cómo era la Venecia del Nuevo Mundo?
3. ¿Quiénes necesitaban sangre?
4. ¿Cuántas personas murieron como ofrendas?
5. Según los aztecas, ¿qué era necesario para una buena vida?

B. ¿a, b o c? Circle the correct answer.

1. Los dioses aztecas eran dioses
   a. alegres.
   b. tristes.
   c. sanguinarios.

2. Tlaloc (line 12) era el dios
   a. del maíz.
   b. de la lluvia.
   c. de la guerra.

3. Según los aztecas, los sacrificios humanos eran
   a. horrorosos.
   b. crueles.
   c. necesarios.

C. Escoge. Choose the appropriate verb and write its imperfect form to complete each sentence.

| ir | hacer | creer | ser |

1. Catalina y Pedro _____ al mercado todos los sábados.

2. Los aztecas _____ en sus dioses importantes.

3. _____ mucho calor en la selva en julio.

4. La Venecia del Nuevo Mundo _____ un paraíso fabuloso.

D. ¡Dibujemos! On a separate sheet of paper, draw the levels of Mexican history that are represented in the Zócalo; today, a great, bustling square flanked by the massive cathedral and the National Palace, in a city of over 18 million people; yesterday, the Venice of the New World . . . ¡un paraíso de canales, puentes, pirámides majestuosas, chinampas y dioses sanguinarios!

CAPÍTULO

Una decisión

17

Antes de leer

Preterite Tense

The preterite is another past tense. It describes an action that happened and was completed at a definite time in the past. While the imperfect tense describes the background action (what was already going on), the preterite tells what happened at a specific time in the past.

To form the preterite of regular **-ar** verbs, the infinitive ending is dropped and the following endings are added to the stem: **-é, -aste, -ó, -amos, -asteis, -aron**.

	hablar
yo	habl**é**
tú	habl**aste**
él, ella, usted	habl**ó**
nosotros, -as	habl**amos**
(vosotros, -as	habl**asteis**)
ellos, ellas, ustedes	habl**aron**

The preterite of regular **-er** and **-ir** verbs is formed by dropping the infinitive endings and adding the following endings: **-í, -iste, -ió, -imos, -isteis, -ieron**.

	comer	vivir
yo	com**í**	viv**í**
tú	com**iste**	viv**iste**
el, ella, usted	com**ió**	viv**ió**
nosotros, -as	com**imos**	viv**imos**
(vosotros, -as	com**isteis**	viv**isteis**)
ellos, ellas, ustedes	com**ieron**	viv**ieron**

Some important verbs that are irregular in the preterite are:

ser ⎫ **ir** ⎭	fui fuiste fue fuimos (fuisteis) fueron
decir	dije dijiste dijo dijimos (dijisteis) dijeron
estar	estuve estuviste estuvo estuvimos estuvisteis estuvieron

Una decisión

"¡Hijos! ¡Escúchenme, por favor!" exclamó el señor Johnson. Toda la familia le prestó atención.°

"Es imposible ver en pocos días todo lo que hay en esta fabulosa ciudad. Hay tantos museos y castillos,
5 el Ballet Folklórico y el sitio más impresionante de todos, el Museo de Antropología. Según todo el mundo,° el museo es una maravilla, una presentación dramática de la historia del indio en México, ¡en tres dimensiones!"

10 "Papá, por favorcito. No quiero ver más museos ahora. Podemos ver el Museo de Antropología después de nuestro viaje a Chiapas y Yucatán", rogó° Pedro, harto° de ser turista y ansioso de salir de la ciudad.

"Sí, sí, Papá. Tenemos que ponernos en camino°

prestó atención: *paid attention*

todo el mundo: *everyone*

rogó: *begged*
harto: *fed up*
ponernos en camino: *hit the road*

15 porque vienen las lluvias", anunció Catalina, también
harta de las atracciones turísticas y deseosa de
acampar en la selva en verdadero territorio indio.

"Bueno. Al volver de Yucatán, con nuestros diarios,
las fotos y experiencias en el mundo de los mayas,
20 podremos° apreciar más el talento artístico que se
exhibe en el museo. Pues, vamos a recoger° la
camioneta° y a prepararnos para el viaje!" dijo la
señora Johnson.

"¡Vámonos ya! Si nos damos prisa° y tenemos
25 suerte, vamos a pasar la noche en nuestras tiendas
de campaña en el valle de Oaxaca!" exclamó Catalina
alegremente.

podremos: *we'll be able to*
recoger: *pick up*
camioneta: *van*

nos damos prisa: *we hurry*

Actividades

A. Preguntas. Answer these questions either orally or in writing on a separate sheet of paper.

1. ¿Por qué es imposible ver todo en la capital?
2. Según todo el mundo, ¿cómo es el Museo de Antropología?
3. ¿Por qué Pedro no quería ver el museo?
4. ¿Por qué era necesario ponerse en camino?
5. ¿Qué iban a recoger y preparar los Johnson?
6. Si los Johnson se dan prisa, ¿dónde van a pasar la noche?

B. Empareja. Draw a line to match each phrase in Column A with a related phrase in Column B.

A	B
1. museos y castillos	**a.** la estación lluviosa
2. la historia del indio	**b.** la camioneta
3. las lluvias	**c.** atracciones turísticas
4. diarios y fotos	**d.** el Museo de Antropología
5. transporte a Yucatán	**e.** del mundo de los mayas

C. ¿Y tú? Answer these questions in complete sentences.

1. Cuando eras pequeño(a), ¿qué hacías generalmente los fines de semana?
2. ¿A qué deportes jugabas?
3. ¿Qué programas de televisión mirabas?
4. ¿Dónde pasaba tu familia las vacaciones?
5. ¿Trabajabas durante el verano a veces?

¿Sabes?

A group of students was gazing in awe at the giant mushroom waterfall that marks the entrance to the Museum of Anthropology. They were overheard saying, "This is the greatest museum in the world! It has real Indian tombs filled with skeletons and treasures of gold, silver, and jade. And life-size figures of all the Indian cultures of Mexico in reconstructed villages with adobe houses and thatched roofs. They show the Indians planting corn, weaving with backstrap looms, making pottery, and building pyramids to their gods. And there's music! Drums made of jaguar skins with deer-antler drum sticks, flutes, trumpets, and rattles. This is my third visit and I can't wait to come back!"

The museum's collection of pre-Hispanic tools and folk art is truly incredible, covering the earliest hunting period of around 10,000 B.C. to the end of the Aztec empire in 1521. Textiles, elaborate jewelry and headdresses, and reproductions of the famous murals of Bonampak and of the Mayan codices are all presented in dramatic displays.

The museum also takes traveling exhibits into remote, rural areas to help today's Indians learn about their past and feel pride in the astonishing accomplishments of their ancestors.

Indian weaver using backstrap loom

La camioneta

18

Antes de leer

Adverbial Phrases: Imperfect

The following adverbial phrases are typical of the kinds of expressions that are used with the imperfect tense.

a veces	sometimes
muchas veces	many times, often
con frecuencia	frequently
generalmente	generally
todos los días	every day
siempre	always
de vez en cuando	every once in a while
cada mes (año, día)	every month (year, day)

Complete each of these sentences with the imperfect form of the verb in brackets.

1. Los Johnson _____ un viaje todos los veranos.
   [hacer]

2. _____ imposible ver todo lo que _____ en esa
   [ser]   [haber]
   ciudad.

3. De vez en cuando Pedro _____ en los dioses sanguinarios.
   [pensar]

4. Con frecuencia Catalina _____ con jaguares.
   [soñar]

5. A veces nosotros _____ al mercado.
   [ir]

La camioneta

Con mucho entusiasmo, la familia fue al mercado
para comprar comida, agua purificada, frutas frescas,
refrescos, gas butano y hielo. La atmósfera era
festiva y ruidosa.

5 "Señorita, ¿desea usted una garganta° de iguana,
un conejo° despellejado° o ajo° para curar el mal de
ojo?"° preguntó una anciana sentada detrás de sus
mercancías.

"No gracias, señora. Hoy no, quizás mañana",
10 respondió Catalina con una expresión de horror.

Después de comprar todas las cosas necesarias, los
Johnson tomaron un taxi a la agencia donde los
esperaba una vieja camioneta. Era amarilla y roja,
con alegres dibujos° de tiburones° pintados a cada
15 lado.

El señor Johnson se puso° pálido.

garganta: *throat*
conejo: *rabbit*
despellejado: *skinned*
ajo: *garlic* • mal de ojo:
evil eye

dibujos: *pictures*
tiburones: *sharks*

se puso: *became*

"Buenos días, señores", dijo el representante de la agencia, un anciano sin dientes.

"Aunque la camioneta es tan vieja como yo, está
20 vivita y coleando!"° exclamó el agente con un ataque de risa.°

vivita y coleando: *alive and kicking*
risa: *laughter*

El señor Johnson tomó las llaves. Su mano temblaba.

"Buena suerte, señores. Si tienen problemas, los
25 Ángeles Verdes* les pueden arreglar todo", aseguró el agente, riéndose a carcajadas.°

riéndose a carcajadas: *howling with laughter*

Los Johnson se miraron alarmados. Tan pronto como pudieron,° metieron° todo el equipo dentro de la camioneta y salieron de la ciudad.

pudieron: *could*
metieron: *put*

---

* **Los Ángeles Verdes** are government-operated pickup trucks that come to the aid of stranded, injured, or hysterical travelers.

Actividades

A. Preguntas. Answer these questions either orally or in writing on a separate sheet of paper.

1. ¿Cómo es la atmósfera en los mercados de México?
2. ¿Qué compraron los Johnson?
3. ¿Qué quería vender a Catalina la anciana en el mercado?
4. ¿Cómo era la camioneta?
5. ¿Cómo reaccionó el señor Johnson al recibir las llaves del representante?

B. ¿Sí o no? Write **sí** if the sentence is true according to the story. If the sentence is false, write **no**; then rewrite the sentence by correcting the underlined words.

1. Los Johnson compraron la camioneta en el mercado.

   _____

2. La garganta de iguana cura el mal de ojo.

   _____

3. Había dibujos de jaguares a cada lado de la camioneta.

   _____

4. Los Johnson estuvieron muy alegres al ver la camioneta pintoresca.

   _____

5. El señor Johnson se puso pálido porque hacía calor.

   _____

C. ¿Para qué sirve? Draw a line to match each item in Column A to its use in Column B.

<table>
<tr><td align="center">A</td><td align="center">B</td></tr>
<tr><td>1. el gas butano</td><td>a. beber</td></tr>
<tr><td>2. el agua purificada</td><td>b. cocinar</td></tr>
<tr><td>3. el hielo</td><td>c. comer</td></tr>
<tr><td>4. las frutas frescas</td><td>d. enfriar</td></tr>
</table>

D. Reread the story and list all the past tense verbs. Give the meaning of each one.

E. ¡Dibujemos! On a separate sheet of paper, draw the VW van, packed and ready to go. Don't forget the agent, the sharks, and the Johnsons!

CAPÍTULO

A Oaxaca

19

Antes de leer

Adverbial Phrases: Preterite

The following adverbial phrases are typical of the kinds of expressions that are used with the preterite tense.

ayer	yesterday
anoche	last night
la semana pasada	last week
el mes pasado	last month
ayer por la tarde	yesterday afternoon
a las dos	at two o'clock

Complete each of these sentences with the preterite form of the verb in brackets.

1. Ayer a las dos los Johnson _____ la camioneta.
   [recoger]

2. Anoche Catalina y su mamá _____ las cosas necesarias.
   [comprar]

3. El mes pasado nosotros _____ en los Estados Unidos.
   [estar]

4. Pedro _____ fotos fabulosas el año pasado.
   [sacar]

5. Ayer por la tarde la señora Johnson _____ al museo.
   [ir]

A Oaxaca

Después de una hora de puro terror en las
glorietas° de la capital, los Johnson estaban
en la carretera° a Oaxaca.

glorietas: *traffic circles*

carretera: *road*

    El paisaje era muy variado. Pasaban por
5 pueblitos llenos de actividad y por regiones
agrícolas con campos de verduras y frutales.
Había valles fértiles donde se cultiva el maíz
desde hace° 6,000 años. Montañas
majestuosas rodeaban los valles y los pueblos

desde hace: *since*

10 pequeños. Era necesario sonar el claxon
constantemente en cada pueblito para abrirse
camino. Había una multitud de burros, vacas,
niños, caballos, guajolotes,° cerdos y
carretillas.° Sobre ellos volaban zopilotes° que

guajolotes: *turkeys*

carretillas: *carts* • zopilotes: *vultures*

15 buscaban animales muertos para comer. Los
topes° en el centro de cada calle añadían más
obstáculos.

topes: *speed bumps*

"¡Qué peligroso!" dijo el señor Johnson.
"¡Es un desafío° estar en el camino porque es   desafío: *challenge*
20 obvio que las calles son el centro de la vida
social!"

Mientras miraban con entusiasmo a los
indios con trajes típicos que caminaban en
fila india en la carretera, Catalina y Pedro
25 comían bocadillos,° tomaban refrescos y   bocadillos: *snacks*
hablaban del paisaje maravilloso de México.
Por fin, después de un día lleno de vistas y
experiencias nuevas, la señora Johnson
exclamó:
30   "¡Miren! ¡Montañas púrpuras! ¡Verdes
valles fértiles! ¡Tuliperos° rojos! ¡Ya estamos   Tuliperos: *tulip trees*
en Oaxaca!"

Actividades

A. Preguntas. Answer these questions either orally or in writing on a separate sheet of paper.

1. ¿Por qué era difícil manejar en la capital de México?
2. Describe el paisaje de la ciudad a Oaxaca.
3. ¿Por qué era complicado pasar por los pueblitos?
4. ¿Qué hacían Catalina y Pedro mientras viajaban?
5. ¿Cómo sabía la señora Johnson que estaban en Oaxaca?

B. Categorías. Cross out the word that does not belong in each category.

1. frutales	verduras	cerdos	maíz
2. guajolotes	claxon	zopilotes	burros
3. valles	montañas	campos	vacas

C. ¿Cómo se dice? Translate these sentences into Spanish.

1. It was midnight when we left.

_____

2. Yesterday afternoon the van traveled through marvelous countryside.

_____

3. We discovered the pyramids last week.

_____

D. Para completar. Complete these sentences in interesting ways that are consistent with the story. Use the preterite or the imperfect.

1. Manejar en la capital de México _____

_____

2. La carretera a Oaxaca _____

_____

3. Anoche a las doce los Johnson _____

_____

4. El mes pasado los indios _____

_____

5. A las siete de la mañana Catalina _____

_____

¿Sabes?

Oaxaca: The dramatic meeting point of two great mountain ranges that shelter fertile valleys where people have lived since the very earliest times. More than 75 percent of the population of Oaxaca is Indian. These people still follow a pattern of life that has barely changed since Cortez's arrival in 1519. Corn or maize (**maíz**) has been grown there for over 6,000 years and is still considered "God's sunbeam"—the root, staff, nourisher, and symbol of eternal life.

Today, the descendants of the Zapotec and Mixtec cultures (whose achievements at Monte Albán and Mitla possibly rivaled those of the Aztec and the Maya) still occupy the same territory, wear the same handwoven indigenous clothing, communicate in the same languages as their ancestors, and continue to leave offerings to their gods in the mountain caves around Oaxaca.

Mayan design

The Voladores (flyers). This daring aerial dance is still performed in villages to honor the Roman Catholic saints, and to ensure a successful harvest. Five men in ceremonial costume climb the 80-foot pole to a tiny platform where one does a hair-raising dance to the music of a fife and drum. At a musical signal, the other four, with ropes attached, hurl themselves into the air and "fly" toward the earth.

CAPÍTULO

El campamento

20

Antes de leer

Helpful Reading Strategies

By now, you are an expert in using strategies that help you read in Spanish. But let's review some of the things that can help you understand the story.

1. Look at the title and make sure you understand what it means.
2. Look at the illustrations and photographs that accompany the reading. What does the art tell you about what you are about to read?
3. Read the comprehension questions and the glossed vocabulary before getting into the reading passage itself.
4. Use all your knowledge of word roots and word families to help make sense of the story without having to depend on your dictionary.
5. As this is an adventure story, follow the Mayan route on your own map; do extra research on various aspects of Indian life and really travel in the van with the Johnson family!

El campamento

La familia buscaba un lugar perfecto al pie de las montañas púrpuras cuando de pronto Pedro exclamó:

"¡Mira, Papá! Hay un bosquecillo cerca de ese río y es un lugar designado para campamentos. Podemos
5 nadar antes de cenar para refrescarnos del calor que hace".

"¡Qué buena idea!" respondió el señor Johnson.

Se estacionaron° y descargaron de la camioneta las cosas necesarias para acampar.

estacionaron: *parked*

10 "Hijos, primero tenemos que armar° las tiendas de campaña", dijo el señor Johnson.

armar: *put up*

"Sí, sí, jefe", contestaron Catalina y Pedro, con el martillo° y las estacas° en la mano.

martillo: *hammer*
estacas: *stakes*

Después de mucha actividad frenética, el
15 campamento estaba listo. Las hamacas estaban atadas° en medio de unos árboles altos. El hornillo,

atadas: *tied*

lleno de gas butano, funcionaba perfectamente y un
rico olor de hamburguesas, frijoles y tortillas llenaba
el aire.

20 "¡A nadar todos!" gritó Catalina, ya en su traje de
baño.

"¡Cuidado, hijos! Hay muchos insectos y víboras° en   víboras: *snakes*
la selva y no sabemos si hay cocodrilos en este río",
advirtió el señor Johnson.

25 "¡Ay, Papá!" dijo Pedro. "Garrapatas,° jejenes,°   garrapatas: *ticks*
víboras y alacranes aquí en el campamento . . . ¡es   jejenes: *gnats*
mucho mejor que estar en un hotel en la ciudad!"

Más tarde, cómodos en los sacos para dormir, los
Johnson dormían como lirones.° No oyeron los gritos   dormían como lirones:
30 de las aves ni de los animales que vagabundeaban   *slept like logs*
por la selva.

Actividades

A. Preguntas. Answer these questions either orally or in writing on a separate sheet of paper.

1. ¿Para qué buscaba la familia un lugar en el valle de Oaxaca?
2. ¿Qué quería hacer Pedro antes de cenar?
3. ¿Qué tiempo hacía?
4. ¿Qué iba a comer la familia?
5. ¿Qué problemas existen en la selva que no existen en un hotel en la ciudad?

B. Categorías. Read the words. Then put the items under the correct categories.

víboras	gas butano	hamburguesas	estacas
tiendas de campaña	garrapatas	hornillo	frijoles
hamacas	alacranes	martillo	jejenes

el campamento   la comida   los animales

_____   _____   _____

_____   _____   _____

_____   _____   _____

_____   _____   _____

C. ¡Dibujemos! Las montañas púrpuras rodeaban los verdes valles fértiles. Los Johnson escogieron un campamento en un bosquecillo cerca del río. Hacía mucho calor y la familia quería nadar antes de cenar. Había una variedad de insectos, víboras y animales salvajes cerca del río.

Copy this map and set up camp! Don't forget:

dos tiendas de campaña
cuatro sacos para dormir
el hornillo
las sartenes
las hamacas
el río
los cocodrilos
los insectos
las víboras

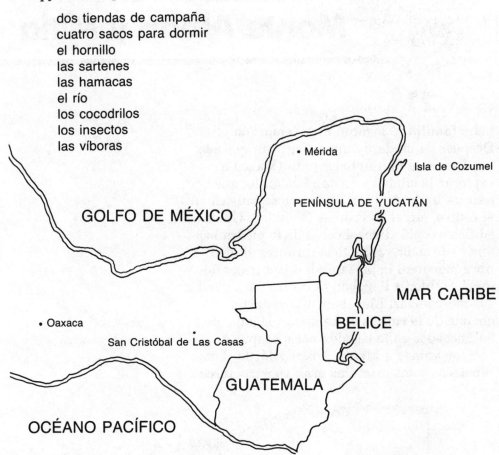

GOLFO DE MÉXICO

• Mérida

Isla de Cozumel

PENÍNSULA DE YUCATÁN

MAR CARIBE

• Oaxaca

San Cristóbal de Las Casas

BELICE

GUATEMALA

OCÉANO PACÍFICO

Monte Albán y Mitla

21

La familia se levantó muy temprano.
Después de un desayuno delicioso preparado
por Pedro, se fueron todos para Oaxaca a
explorar la ciudad colonial. El Zócalo, que
5 parecía un jardín, con un kiosco de música en
el centro, era el corazón de la ciudad. Había
edificios espléndidos, hechos de la piedra local
que es de color verde. Restaurantes al aire
libre rodeaban la plaza. Indios con trajes de
10 muchos colores llegaban al centro para vender
sus mercancías. Llevaban sus productos
encima de la cabeza en canastas de paja° o   paja: *straw*
balanceados en la espalda por mecapales.°   mecapales: *forehead harnesses*

"Hoy vamos a Monte Albán y Mitla. Los
15 zapotecas y los mixtecas eran constructores

fabulosos. Las ruinas allá son monumentos a
sus culturas", dijo la señora Johnson.

Seis kilómetros al suroeste de Oaxaca, en
lo alto de unas colinas, los Johnson vieron un
20 panorama magnífico. ¡Monte Albán! Alrededor
de la plaza central había pirámides, templos,
plataformas y una cancha° para el juego de   cancha: *court*
pelota llamado Pok-a-Tok.

"En una de las tumbas subterráneas, la
25 número 7, se encontraron tesoros increíbles:
anillos,° máscaras, collares de perlas,   anillos: *rings*
cascabeles° de oro y también unos huesos° de   cascabeles: *bells* • huesos: *bones*
jaguar adornados con diseños tallados",°   diseños tallados: *carved designs*
explicó el señor Johnson. "Todos estos objetos
30 especiales eran utilizados en el viaje largo".

"Y cuando los zapotecas abandonaron su
ciudad ceremonial, los mixtecas, escultores
magníficos del metal y de la piedra,
construyeron sus propias ciudades, usando
35 como base las estructuras de los zapotecas",
añadió Catalina.

Actividades

A. Preguntas. Answer these questions either orally or in writing on a separate sheet of paper.

1. ¿Cómo es la ciudad de Oaxaca?
2. ¿Quiénes fueron los arquitectos de Monte Albán y Mitla?
3. ¿Qué se encontró en una de las tumbas subterráneas de Monte Albán?
4. ¿Para qué ponían los indios objectos especiales en las tumbas?
5. ¿Qué hicieron los mixtecas al encontrar las ruinas abandonadas por los zapotecas?

B. Empareja. Draw a line to match each Spanish phrase in Column A with its English meaning in Column B.

A	B
1. cascabeles de oro	a. forehead harnesses
2. trajes típicos	b. death
3. mecapales	c. underground tombs
4. tumbas subterráneas	d. native dress
5. el viaje largo	e. golden bells

C. Frases originales. Write a complete sentence in Spanish about each of these topics.

1. el Zócalo

_____

2. los mecapales

_____

3. las tumbas subterráneas

_____

¿Sabes?

When Alfonso Caso, the famous Mexican archaeologist, entered subterranean tomb number 7, he gasped in wonder at his discovery. A translucent, white amphora* made of **tecali** (a type of onyx) glistened amidst piles of human bones. Some arm bones wore beautiful bracelets. There were skulls decorated with turquoise, and the tomb floor was covered with pearls and golden beads carved in the shape of turtles or jaguars. In a sitting position among all these fantastic treasures were nine corpses (possibly representing the Nine Lords of the underworld) who were to accompany the dead ruler on his long journey.

The Mixtecs were masters of the art of metal sculpture. Their craft included smelting, welding, inlaying, and embossing beautiful designs onto thin sheets of gold or silver. They also used the "lost wax method" (still used today), in which clay is covered with beeswax, then modeled and molded into the desired shape, covered with clay, and heated. After the wax melts it is poured out, and molten metal is poured in and left to harden.

* A tall jar with a narrow neck and base, and two handles; also used by the ancient Greeks and Romans

El Cañón del Sumidero

22

"Papá, en ruta a Tuxtla Gutiérrez, ¿podemos
explorar el Cañón del Sumidero en lancha?"° sugirió
Catalina. "Hay animales en la región que están casi
extintos. ¡Animales que vivían en los tiempos de los
5 mayas!"

"¿Qué tipo de animales?" preguntó la señora
Johnson.

"Hay gatos monteses,° tapires, jabalíes,° ocelotes y
víboras peligrosas como el coralillo y la boa. Debemos
10 turnarnos con los binoculares para verlos todos",
añadió Catalina.

La carretera a Tuxtla era muy montañosa y
estrecha, con curvas peligrosas. No había barreras,°
solamente unas filas de palos° rectos que delineaban

lancha: *boat*

gatos monteses:
mountain lions
jabalíes: *boars*

barreras: *fences*
palos: *sticks*

15 el borde del camino. A los camioneros° les gustaba
mucho pasar a los otros camiones y coches en las
altas curvas peligrosas. Era un juego de suerte, de
azar, como una "ruleta rusa".

    "Allá está el embarcadero° Cahuaré, donde se
20 alquilan° las lanchas", dijo el señor Johnson.

    "¡Qué horror!" exclamó Pedro al mirar los
precipicios que bordeaban el río Grijalvo. ¡Tienen una
altura aproximada de 1,000 metros!"

    El guía explicaba mientras controlaba la lancha:
25 "Este cañón es el más profundo de las Américas. Es
aquí donde se suicidaron los indios chiapas para
evitar la esclavitud° de los españoles". La lancha
pasaba cerca de grutas oscuras entre abismos rocosos.
Sobre la superficie del profundo río volaban garzas°
30 blancas y cientos de mariposas coloridas.

    Los fantasmas de los indios chiapas, la presencia
de animales raros, la circulación de los aguiluchos,°
garzas y mariposas . . . todo era como un sueño. Un
cocodrilo siniestro que miraba fijamente la lancha
35 desde la orilla° del río, de repente volvió al agua.

camioneros: *truck drivers*

embarcadero: *dock*
se alquilan: *rent*

esclavitud: *slavery*

garzas: *herons*

aguiluchos: *eaglets*

orilla: *bank*

Actividades

A. Preguntas. Answer these questions either orally or in writing on a separate sheet of paper.

1. ¿Qué animales viven todavía en el Cañón del Sumidero?
2. ¿Cómo era la carretera a Tuxtla?
3. ¿Qué es Cahuaré?
4. Describe el cañón.
5. ¿Cómo escaparon los indios chiapas de los españoles?

B. Empareja. Draw a line to match each item in Column A with its explanation in Column B.

A	B
1. tapires, jabalíes	a. aves del cañón
2. Cahuaré	b. el embarcadero
3. la muerte de los indios chiapas	c. víboras peligrosas
4. garzas, aguiluchos	d. el suicidio
5. el coralillo, la boa	e. animales raros

C. ¿Cómo se dice? Translate these sentences into Spanish.

1. The precipices of the canyon border on the Grijalvo River.

_____

2. Let's look for the almost-extinct animals.

_____

3. The Chiapa Indians didn't want to become slaves of the Spaniards.

_____

D. ¡Dibujemos! On a separate sheet of paper, draw your exploration of the Cañón del Sumidero by boat, remembering the steep, rocky walls, the almost-extinct animals, and the ghosts of the desperate Chiapa Indians. You may also want to model in clay, papier mâché, or plaster of Paris some of the animals and birds that flourished in the time of the Mayas.

CAPÍTULO

San Cristóbal de Las Casas

23

La camioneta vieja, cargada hasta el techo, todavía
funcionaba muy bien, gracias a los dioses. A veces
tenía dificultad al subir las montañas y al escaparse
de los camiones locos y de los derrumbes.° Los dibujos   derrumbes: *landslides*
5 de los tiburones en cada lado de la camioneta
provocaban miradas curiosas de los indios que
caminaban en fila india por la carretera. Llevaban
huipiles* o ponchos de distintos colores luminosos.
Todos iban acompañados de perros, cabras, borregos°   borregos: *sheep*
10 y gallinas. De vez en cuando, se paraban para charlar
o vender sus mercancías.

---

* **huipil**—a loose-fitting embroidered or brocaded blouse woven and worn by
Indian women of Mexico for thousands of years. The complex designs affirm
the wearer's identity and place in the cosmos.

"Ya llegamos a San Cristóbal, Mamá", exclamó
Catalina. Todos admiraron la preciosa ciudad rodeada
de montañas altas. Había casas de muchos colores
15 con techos de tejas° rojas. La Catedral, el Templo de   tejas: *tiles*
Santo Domingo con un altar de oro y el Museo de
Na-Bolom† eran centros de mucho interés. El
mercado indio, con representantes de los pueblos
indígenas, cada uno con un traje diferente, llamó la
20 atención de los Johnson.
   La familia bajó de la camioneta y caminó por el
mercado al aire libre. El sonido de la lengua tzotzil
llenaba el aire. Indios de cada pueblo estaban
sentados detrás de sus montones de mercancía. Ellos
25 regateaban° en voces animadas, tratando de vender   regateaban: *bargained*
sus productos por más dinero. Los mercados son
ejemplos vivos de los trajes, las lenguas, la comida y
las supersticiones de los indios.
   "Papá, ¿es verdad que se practica la brujería°   brujería: *witchcraft*
30 aquí?" preguntó Pedro, mirando con sospecha un
puesto° con colibríes° muertos y ranas° secas.   puesto: *stall* • colibríes:
hummingbirds • ranas:
frogs

_____
† **Na-Bolom**—House of the Jaguar

Actividades

A. Preguntas. Answer these questions either orally or in writing on a separate sheet of paper.

1. ¿Qué dificultades tenía la camioneta?
2. ¿Cómo reaccionaban los indios a los dibujos de los tiburones?
3. ¿Para qué se paraban los indios en la carretera?
4. ¿Cómo es San Cristóbal?
5. ¿Qué pensó Pedro al ver los colibríes muertos?

B. ¿Cuál no va? Cross out the word that does not belong in each group.

1. catedrales	museos	tejas	templos
2. trajes	huipiles	ponchos	techos
3. cabras	lenguas	borregos	perros
4. español	tzotzil	inglés	sonido

C. ¿a, b o c? Circle the correct answer.

1. La camioneta tenía dificultad al
   a. caminar en fila india.
   b. vender sus productos.
   c. escaparse de los derrumbes.

2. San Cristóbal es un
   a. techo rojo.
   b. pueblo indígena.
   c. puesto.

3. El mercado indio revela
   a. la contaminación del aire.
   b. la vida diaria de los indios.
   c. las casas de muchos colores.

¿Sabes?

Brujo,-a means *sorcerer* or *witch*. **Brujería** is *witchcraft* or *magic*. The owl, associated with mystery and death in Indian lore, is sometimes known as a **bruja.** Some of the paraphernalia used in witchcraft are: chickens and deer eyes (powerful amulets against **mal de ojo**), dolls made from the victim's clothing, and herbs, toads, dried hummingbird charms, incense, and snake skins.

Curanderos,-as are shaman-priests or witch doctors who have been summoned in their dreams to the caves of the Ancestors (father/mother spirit beings), who watch over their children in the villages. In dreams, those summoned are given "second sight," that is, special knowledge about curative herbs, amulets, and prayers to use in curing the sick. They are also taught how to play the harp, guitar, and violin, a vital part of any curing ritual.

"Soul loss" and "evil eye" are the leading causes of Tzotzil illness. Witches or pagan gods can capture people's souls by stealing their "companion animal spirit." Everyone has a companion animal, which lives inside the mountain and is protected by the Ancestors. The personality of the individual is often reflected in the animal chosen as a companion. Which animal would YOU choose as a spirit companion? Why?

The **curandero** is the only one who can tell whether it was witchcraft or a person's own misdeeds that caused the soul loss. The sacrifice of a black chicken, in exchange for the freedom of the animal companion, is performed in elaborate, mystical ceremonies. Following the sacrifice, the **curandero** calls the lost soul through a hollow gourd. The patient recovers when his or her soul is returned to the body.

> **Grano de oro:** Compasses are magical because they guide us in our travels. It's no coincidence that the Spanish word for *compass* is **brújula!**

San Juan de Chamula

24

La brujería existe en todas partes de
México. En los mercados se puede comprar
hierbas medicinales, incienso, gallinas negras
para sacrificar y amuletos especiales para
5 ponerse en contacto con los dioses.

"Ahora vamos a visitar San Juan de
Chamula y Zinacantán. Los indios allá tienen
costumbres raras y tradiciones antiguas que
todavía gobiernan su vida. Pero, ¡cuidado! No
10 se permite sacar fotos porque los indios
piensan que la cámara captura el alma de la
persona", advirtió° el señor Johnson.   advirtió: *warned*

La plaza de San Juan de Chamula estaba
llena de indios con ropa típica, hablando en
15 tzotzil. Estaba muy nublado, con el humo° de   humo: *smoke*

copal, un incienso dulce y pesado. A cada
lado de la plaza había dos iglesias
impresionantes, una blanca decorada con
serpentinas de festival y otra cuya entrada
20 estaba pintada de turquesa con diseños
bonitos. Dentro de esa iglesia iluminada por
cientos de velas,° había estatuas de santos   velas: *candles*
católicos, todos vestidos con huipiles
antiguos, tejidos° por los mejores artistas de   tejidos: *woven*
25 la región. Una voz alta e hipnótica penetraba
el denso humo. Era el curandero que trataba
de devolver° el alma perdida del enfermo que   devolver: *bring back*
estaba acostado° sobre ramas° de pino. Una   acostado: *lying down* • ramas:
gallina negra aleteaba° cerca del paciente.   *branches*
                                                aleteaba: *was flapping*
30   "¡Qué ceremonia tan misteriosa!" exclamó
Catalina al salir de la iglesia. "Me hace
temblar el pensar en el poder de los
curanderos y de las creencias mayas".
   En la camioneta de nuevo, los Johnson
35 seguían la ruta maya hacia Palenque, el
lugar místico donde los sacerdotes° y los jefes   sacerdotes: *priests*
se reunían con los dioses.

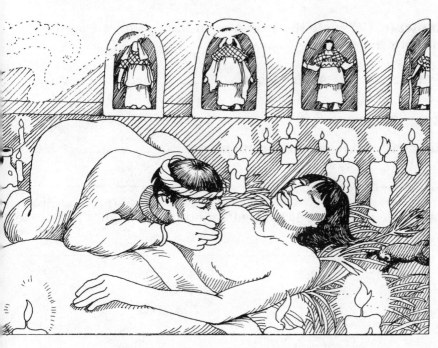

Actividades

A. Preguntas. Answer these questions either orally or in writing on a separate sheet of paper.

1. ¿Para qué sirven las hierbas y gallinas negras que se venden en el mercado?
2. ¿Por qué no se permite sacar fotos en San Juan de Chamula?
3. ¿Cómo era la plaza de San Juan de Chamula?
4. Describe el interior de la iglesia turquesa.
5. ¿Qué quería hacer el curandero?

B. Empareja. Draw a line to match each phrase in Column A with a related phrase in Column B.

A	B
1. denso humo	a. el curandero
2. voz hipnótica	b. santos católicos
3. huipiles antiguos	c. copal
4. serpentinas de festival	d. iglesia blanca

C. Para completar. Complete the sentences in interesting ways that are consistent with the story.

1. La brujería me hace temblar porque _____

_____

2. San Juan de Chamula es interesante porque _____

_____

3. Las estatuas de santos católicos llevaban huipiles antiguos porque

_____

D. ¡Dibujemos! ¿Eres curandero,-a? On a separate sheet of paper, draw the main plaza in San Juan de Chamula. Go to the Indian market and buy all of the items you will need to cure your patient, who is suffering from **el mal de ojo** and **el alma perdida**. Add these items to your drawing.

*Ancient designs on a **huipil**. Each design is significant, and proclaims the wearer's place in the cosmos.*

CAPÍTULO

Palenque

25

"¡Qué maravilla!" gritó el señor Johnson al ver la ciudad magnífica de Palenque. Alrededor de los templos impresionantes y de las plataformas decoradas, había colinas con árboles altos llenos de
5 monos, loros y otras aves tropicales.

"Vamos a subir al Templo de las Inscripciones", sugirió Pedro, deseoso de encontrar la famosa escalera secreta que baja al fondo de la pirámide donde está la tumba de Pacal.*
10 Después de siglos de haber estado cerrada, aunque estaba bien iluminada, la escalera era húmeda y misteriosa. Catalina y Pedro bajaron los escalones mojados.° De repente, se encontraron° en un espacio

mojados: *wet* • se encontraron: *they found themselves*

* A royal Mayan chief (A.D. 700)

angosto,° sin aire, enfrente de la lápida° de la tumba.

15 "¡Qué emocionante!" susurraron los dos.

"Los arqueólogos encontraron al pobre Pacal
cubierto de jade y turquesa. También llevaba una
máscara de jade, y hasta en su boca había un
pedacito de jade para la comida eterna", explicó
20 Catalina.

"¡Me da escalofrío!" exclamó Pedro. "¡Vámonos de
aquí!"

Mientras exploraban el resto del área, los Johnson
vieron a unos indios extraños de pelo negro y muy
25 largo, y vestidos con largas túnicas blancas. Parecían
de otro mundo, como figuras de la escultura maya.

"Son lacandones, descendientes de los mayas.
Están casi extintos por la destrucción de la selva
tropical, su hogar físico y espiritual", explicó el señor
30 Johnson.

"Los lacandones todavía llevan incienso y comida
al dios del sol, que según ellos, vive en el templo de
Yaxchilán en la profundidad de la selva lacandona",
añadió la señora Johnson.

angosto: *narrow*
lápida: *cover*

Actividades

A. Preguntas. Answer these questions either orally or in writing on a separate sheet of paper.

1. Describe Palenque.
2. ¿Qué había al fondo de la escalera secreta?
3. ¿Cómo reaccionaron Catalina y Pedro al ver la lápida?
4. ¿Qué descubrieron los arqueólogos?
5. ¿Quiénes son los lacandones?

B. Empareja. Draw a line to match each phrase in Column A with a related word or phrase in Column B.

A	B
1. escalones mojados	a. Palenque
2. la comida eterna	b. descendientes de los mayas
3. los lacandones	c. jade
4. el Templo de las Inscripciones	d. escalera secreta

C. ¿Sí o no? Write **sí** if the sentence is true according to the story. If the sentence is false, write **no**; then rewrite the sentence by correcting the underlined words.

1. Alrededor de los templos impresionantes había <u>escaleras secretas</u>.

_____

2. En la boca de Pacal había un <u>bocadillo</u> para la comida eterna.

_____

3. Los lacandones son <u>figuras de la escultura maya</u>.

_____

¿Sabes?

Tzotzil is one of the languages spoken by the Indians in Chiapas. Also called "Batz'i K'op" (true speech), it has a very complex grammar with odd, glottal sounds that can give different meanings to each word.

As you already know, corn is the staff of life in the pueblos, and is the basic ingredient of tortillas. In Tzotzil, the importance of the tortilla is demonstrated by the variety of names given to it. When it is cooked, from what kind of corn it is made, and to whom it belongs are all categories that have special names. "My tortilla" is *kot* while "your tortilla" is *avot*. A "slept tortilla" (one made the night before) is a *vayemvah*. Tortillas made from fresh corn, as opposed to dried, boiled kernels, are *ach vah*. Corn of each color and growth stage has a different flavor and a distinct name.

If a Mayan girl breaks with tradition and refuses to make tortillas, leaves from a local tree—the *memela*—are heated on the griddle and pressed between her hands as punishment.

CAPÍTULO

Uxmal y Chichén Itzá

26

"¡Despiértense,° hijos!" gritó la señora Johnson. "Tenemos que ponernos en camino. ¡La península de Yucatán nos espera!"

Era muy temprano y hacía mucho calor. La familia
5 se levantó° inmediatamente y empacó la camioneta para el viaje a Yucatán.

Después de muchas horas de camino, viajando por campos de maguey* que rodeaban los pueblos indígenas, la camioneta llegó a Uxmal, un símbolo
10 fabuloso de la grandeza del imperio maya. Dos grandes pirámides decoradas en mosaico dominaban la plaza. Chac, el dios de la lluvia, con la trompa larga de un elefante, estaba representado en las máscaras que adornaban la fachada de los templos
15 impresionantes.

Aunque querían pasar más tiempo en explorar los alrededores° de Uxmal, los Johnson subieron a la

***

* Spiky cactus used in making rope

Despiértense: *Wake up*

se levantó: *got up*

alrededores: *surroundings*

camioneta y continuaron su viaje hacia la costa este
de Yucatán.

20 "¡Chichén Itzá! ¡Qué sensacional!" exclamó
Catalina mientras corría hacia el Templo de
Kukulcán.† Dos enormes estatuas de piedra de
serpientes emplumadas estaban a lado y lado de la
escalera empinada del templo. Adentro estaba el
25 Trono del Jaguar Rojo, con ojos de jade y dientes de
concha.° También había un Chac Mool.   concha: *shell*

"¿Conocen ustedes a Chac Mool?" preguntó el señor
Johnson al ver una extraña estatua de piedra, la de
un hombre medio inclinado.
30 "Sí, Papá", contestó Pedro. "En un receptáculo
dentro de su estómago, los indios ponían los corazones
(todavía palpitando) que habían sacado de personas
vivas!"

"Si ustedes quieren ver más evidencia de los
35 sacrificios humanos, podemos visitar el Cenote
Sagrado,‡ que está cerca", sugirió la señora Johnson.

Con los ojos como platos, dijo Catalina: "Gracias,
Mamá, pero me gustan más los indios vivos que los
muertos. ¡Vamos a Tulum!"

---

† The Mayan name for Quetzalcoatl, the chief diety

‡ Sacred Well. Archaeologists have discovered a treasure trove at the bottom
of this well: gold, copper, fine jade, as well as the bones of sacrificial victims
of all ages.

Actividades

A. Preguntas. Answer these questions either orally or in writing on a separate sheet of paper.

1. ¿Por qué se levantaron temprano los Johnson?
2. ¿Cómo es Uxmal?
3. ¿A quién representa la trompa del elefante?
4. Describe el Templo de Kukulcán.
5. ¿Para qué servían los Chac Mool?

B. ¿a, b o c? Circle the correct answer.

1. **Yucatán** is
   a. a city.
   b. a pyramid.
   c. a peninsula.

2. **El dios de la lluvia** is
   a. Kukulcán.
   b. Quetzalcoatl.
   c. Chac.

3. **Chac Mool** is
   a. a stomach.
   b. a receptacle.
   c. a beating heart.

4. **El Trono del Jaguar Rojo** has eyes of
   a. shell.
   b. jade.
   c. gold.

C. ¡Construyamos! With modeling clay or papier mâché, make either the Throne of the Red Jaguar, a Chac Mool, plumed serpent heads, or the Sacred Well. Or if you prefer, draw the Temple of Kukulcán, with its narrow stairway into secret chambers where the Red Jaguar and Chac Mool are waiting.

Skull platform, Tzompantli, at Chichén Itzá. There is doubt as to whether the winners or the losers were beheaded at the end of the ball game, Pok-a-Tok.

CAPÍTULO

El último día

27

Después de unas horas de viaje, el señor
Johnson exclamó: "¡Miren el color del mar
Caribe! ¡Estamos en Tulum!"

Estacionaron la camioneta cerca de la
5 entrada de la fortaleza magnífica de Tulum.
En lo alto de un precipicio que da al mar
Caribe, la ciudad maya de Tulum está
rodeada por murallas° de defensa que daban   murallas: *walls*
protección contra los invasores. Arriba de la
10 puerta principal del castillo, hay una estatua
misteriosa, la de un dios zambulléndose.°   zambulléndose: *diving*

"Podría ser un símbolo de la decadencia de
los mayas", profetizó la señora Johnson.

Después de explorar la fortaleza, los
15 Johnson nadaron en las aguas cristalinas del
Caribe. También pensaban tristemente en el
safari que estaba por terminar.

"¡Qué viaje tan inolvidable!" exclamó
Catalina. "Hemos subido° pirámides y
20 templos. Aprendimos a leer unos jeroglíficos.
Seguimos las huellas° de animales salvajes
en nuestros campamentos".

"Y conocimos a los dioses mayas. Podemos
reconocer los dialectos y los trajes distintos
25 de los pueblos indígenas", añadió Pedro, con
una expresión nostálgica.

"¡Atención, por favor!" exclamó el señor
Johnson. "Mientras viajamos al aeropuerto,
su mamá va a leernos sobre la llegada de los
30 españoles".

"Una flotilla de enormes barcos—que
parecían montañas con alas, según los
indios—atracó° en las playas. De repente,
bestias sobrenaturales con inmensos cuerpos,
35 con crines° y colas° fantásticas
desembarcaron a galope tendido.° Montados
en estos animales espantosos° venían
extranjeros ruidosos con trajes de metal, con
lanzas llameantes° que mataron a los indios".

Hemos subido: *We have climbed*

huellas: *tracks*

atracó: *landed*

crines: *manes* • colas: *tails*
a galope tendido: *at full speed*
espantosos: *terrifying*

llameantes: *flaming*

Actividades

A. Preguntas. Answer these questions either orally or in writing on a separate sheet of paper.

1. Según la señora Johnson, ¿qué significa la estatua misteriosa en Tulum?
2. Después de investigar la fortaleza, ¿qué hicieron los Johnson?
3. ¿Cuáles fueron unas experiencias de los Johnson durante el safari?
4. Describe la llegada de los españoles.
5. ¿Por qué eran espantosos para los indios los animales que tenían los españoles?

B. Empareja. Draw a line to match each phrase in Column A with a related word or phrase in Column B.

A	B
1. bestias sobrenaturales	a. la decadencia de los mayas
2. las murallas	b. caballos
3. enormes barcos	c. la defensa
4. las huellas	d. soldados españoles
5. la estatua misteriosa	e. animales salvajes

C. ¿Y tú? Discuss these questions in class—¡en español!

1. ¿Cómo reaccionas tú a una cultura nueva?
2. Al conocer a extranjeros, ¿cuál es tu primera reacción?
3. ¿Tratas de comprender las costumbres, las religiones o los idiomas que son diferentes a los que conoces?
4. En tu opinión, ¿tenían los españoles derecho a destruir otra civilización para imponer la de ellos?
5. ¿Qué quieres hacer con tu vida? Explica por qué.
6. ¿Cuál es la causa de la tensión que existe en la vida moderna? ¿La desintegración de la familia? ¿La amenaza de una guerra nuclear? ¿El terrorismo en el mundo?

7. ¿Qué opinas de la relación entre las enfermedades de hoy y la tensión?

8. ¿Tienen valor las ceremonias curativas de los curanderos?

D. ¡Dibujemos! Animales, insectos y aves de la selva: Draw as many of these creatures as you can. Choose your favorites.

el aguilucho	el jaguar
el alacrán	el jején
la araña	el loro
la boa	la mariposa
el borrego	el mono
el burro	el murciélago
el caballo	el ocelote
la cabra	el pez
el cerdo	el perro
el cocodrilo	el quetzal
el colibrí	la rana
el coralillo	la serpiente
la gallina	la tarántula
el gallo	el tapir
la garza	el tiburón
el gato montés	la vaca
el guajolote	la víbora
el jabalí	el zopilote

¿Sabes?

An extraordinary civilization, the Mayas developed a calendar of 365 days similar to our calendar of today. Without astronomical instruments, calculators, computers, or telescopes, they could predict eclipses and understand the movement of the stars and planets. They had an elaborate numerical system of bars and dots: each bar represented the number *five*; each dot was the equivalent of *one*. They invented the concept of the zero.

1	2	3	4	5		6	7	8	9	10
•	• •	• • •	• • • •	▬		▬ over •	▬ over • •	▬ over • • •	▬ over • • • •	▬ over ▬

They lumped the years into cycles, with each cycle twenty times the cycle before it. They even had hieroglyphic signs for cyclical units.

| KATUN 20 YEARS | BAKTUN 400 YEARS | PICTUN 8000 YEARS | CALABTUN 160,000 YEARS | KINCHILTUN 3,200,000 YEARS | ALAUTUN 64,000,000 YEARS |

Mayan gods were glorified in sculpture, murals, and in the construction of massive, magnificently adorned temples and pyramids, all achieved without tools or beasts of burden. The horse was unknown. Stelae, or commemorative stones, had intricately sculpted hieroglyphics depicting daily rituals, as well as ruling dynasties and the Mayan link to the gods.

Due to the almost complete destruction of the civilization by the Spanish in their determination to "Christianize the savages," archaeologists of today are only now beginning to understand the hieroglyphic codes. They continue to uncover splendid cities buried deep below the relentless jungle.

Spanish-English Vocabulary

The following Spanish-English vocabulary list contains most of the words and expressions that appear in Mayan Safari. *The numbers after each entry indicate the page on which the word or expression is first presented.*

A

a to, at, by *2*
  a galope tendido at full speed *139*
a veces sometimes *96*
abandonar to abandon *115*
el abismo abyss *119*
abordar to get on board *37*
el abrazo hug *47*
el abrelatas can opener *61*
abrir to open *104*
abrochar to fasten *42*
absolutamente absolutely *87*
aburrido,-a boring *11*
acampar to camp *30*
acompañar to accompany *76*
acostarse to lie down *127*
acostumbrarse to become accustomed *71*
la actividad activity *3*
adentro inside *135*
la admiración admiration *87*
el adobe sun-dried brick *58*
¿adónde? where (to)? *6*
adornar to decorate *115*

advertir (ie) to warn *111*
el aeropuerto airport *30*
la agencia agency *98*
el, la agente agent *99*
agrícola agricultural *104*
el agua water *98*
el ajo garlic *98*
el aguilucho eaglet *119*
ahora now *126*
el aire air *111*
  al aire libre open air *114*
el ajo garlic *98*
la ala wing *139*
el alacrán scorpion *8*
alarmado,-a alarmed *99*
alegre happy *32*
alegremente happily *71*
alegría happiness *64*
aletear to flutter *127*
allá over there *119*
el alma soul *126*
alquilar to rent *119*
alrededor de around *115*
el altavoz loudspeaker *37*
alto,-a tall *8*
la altura altitude *63*
amable amiable, kind *53*

amarillo,-a yellow *98*
americano,-a American *23*
el, la amigo,-a friend *71*
el amuleto amulet, charm *126*
añadir to add *86*
el año year *16*
el, la anciano,-a old person *98*
angosto,-a narrow *131*
el anillo ring *115*
animado,-a lively *46*
anoche last night *102*
ansioso,-a anxious *92*
antes before *1*
antiguo,-a ancient, old *59*
anunciar to announce *37*
apreciar to appreciate *93*
aprender to learn *139*
aproximado,-a approximate *119*
aquí here *24*
la araña spider *8*
el árbol tree *59*
armar to put up *110*
la arma weapon *19*
el, la arqueólogo,-a archeologist *43*
la arquitectura architecture *58*
arreglar to repair *99*
¡Arriba! Come on! *37*
artístico,-a artistic *93*
asegurar to assure *99*
el asiento seat *42*
así thus, so *77*
el aspecto appearance *37*
atacar to attack *44*
el ataque attack *99*
aterrador terrifying *22*
aterrizar to land *49*
la atmósfera atmosphere *98*
atracar to moor *139*
atrapar to trap *65*
aunque although *24*
la ave bird *2*
el, la aventurero,-a adventurer *8*
el avión airplane *18*
ayer yesterday *102*
la azafata stewardess *42*
el azar chance *119*
azteca Aztec *77*

B

bajar to descend, get off *47*
bajo,-a under *87*
balancear to balance *114*
el banco bank *77*
barato,-a inexpensive *77*
el barco boat *139*
la barrera fence, barrier *118*
la base base *115*
el baúl trunk *70*
el béisbol baseball *11*
la bestia beast *139*
bien good, well *51*
bienvenido,-a welcome *52*
los binoculares binoculars *12*
blanco,-a white *119*
la boa boa constrictor *118*
la boca mouth *131*
el bocadillo snack *105*
el bolillo roll *80*
bonito,-a pretty *59*
el borde border *119*
bordear to border *119*
el borrego sheep *122*
el bosquecillo small forest *110*
el botiquín first-aid kit *24*
el brazo arm *48*
brillante brilliant *86*
la brujería witchcraft *123*
brujo,-a sorcerer/witch *125*
la brújula compass *125*
bueno,-a good, fine *24*
el burro burro *64*
buscar to look for *2*
el butano butane *33*

C

el caballo horse *104*
la cabeza head *25*
la cabra goat *58*
la cacofonía cacophony *76*
cada each *12*
Cahuaré dock in the Sumidero Canyon *119*
la calle street *58*

caliente hot *80*
el calor heat *16*
cambiar to exchange, change *46*
la cámera camera *12*
caminar to walk *87*
el camino trail, route *92*
el camión truck *64*
el, la camionero,-a truck
  driver *119*
la camioneta van *93*
el campamento campsite *28*
la campana bell *64*
el campo field *104*
el canal canal *86*
la canasta basket *114*
la cancha court *115*
el cañón canyon *118*
el capítulo chapter *1*
capturar to capture *126*
la carcajada loud laughter *99*
cargar to load *122*
el Caribe The Caribbean *138*
la carne meat *5*
carnívoro,-a meat-eating *2*
la carretera highway, road *104*
la carretilla cart *104*
la casa house *58*
el cascabel small bell *115*
casi almost *64*
el caso case *42*
el castillo castle *92*
católico,-a Catholic *127*
cenar to eat supper *110*
el cenote water well *135*
el centro center *78*
cerca de near *30*
el cerdo pig *58*
la ceremonia ceremony *127*
cerrar (ie) to close *130*
ciento hundred *119*
el cinturón belt *42*
la circulación circulation *119*
la ciudad city *65*
la civilización civilization *43*
la clave key *46*
el claxon horn *64*
el coche car *119*

el cocodrilo crocodile *111*
codicioso,-a greedy *81*
el cognado cognate *1*
la cola tail *139*
el colectivo taxi van *77*
el colibrí hummingbird *123*
la colina hill *43*
el collar necklace *115*
comentar to comment *53*
comer to eat *33*
la comida food *29*
como as, like *8*
¿cómo? how, what *6*
  ¿Cómo se dice? How do you
    say? *21*
cómodo,-a comfortable *111*
completamente completely *8*
completar to complete *128*
comprar to buy *18*
comprender to understand *140*
con with *2*
  con frecuencia frequently *96*
la concha shell *135*
el concierto concert *78*
el conejo rabbit *98*
conocer to know *135*
constantemente constantly *104*
el constructor builder *114*
construir to build *115*
el contacto contact *126*
la contaminación pollution *64*
contento,-a happy *29*
contestar to answer *13*
continuar to continue *43*
contra against *13*
el contraste contrast *58*
controlar to control *119*
el copal incense *127*
el coralillo coral snake *118*
el corazón heart *76*
correr to run *135*
Cortés, Hernán Spanish
  conqueror *80*
la cosa thing *98*
la costa coast *135*
la costumbre custom *126*
crear to create *64*

la creencia belief *127*
creer to believe *84*
la crin mane *139*
cristalino,-a crystal clear *138*
el crucigrama crossword puzzle *32*
cruel cruel *87*
¿cuál,-es? which? *38*
¿cuánto,-a,-os,-as? how much, how many? *75*
cuatro four *33*
cubierto,-a (cubrir) covered *42*
el cuerpo body *139*
la cueva cave *8*
cuidado careful *16*
cultivar to cultivate *104*
la cultura culture *115*
el, la curandero,-a witch doctor *125*
curar to cure *98*
curioso,-a curious *122*
la curva curve *119*
cuya whose *127*

CH

Chac Mool stone statue *135*
el chaleco salvavidas life jacket *42*
charlar to talk *122*
los chiapas natives of Chiapas, Mexican state bordering Guatemala *119*
Chichén Itzá major Mayan site in Yucatan *135*
la chinampa floating garden *83*

D

dar to give *47*
  darse prisa to hurry *93*
de of, from *2*
  de nuevo again *127*
  de pronto suddenly *110*
  de repente suddenly *12*
  de vez en cuando from time to time *96*
debajo de under *42*
deber should *71*

la decadencia decline *138*
decorar to decorate *70*
dedicar to dedicate *39*
la defensa defense *138*
delinear to outline *118*
demasiado,-a too much *64*
denso,-a dense *43*
dentro inside *99*
el deporte sport *94*
el derecho right *81*
el derrumbe landslide *122*
el desafío challenge *5*
la desaparición disappearance *46*
el desayuno breakfast *80*
descansar to rest *71*
descargar to unload *110*
el descendiente descendent *131*
descifrar to decipher *46*
desconocido,-a unknown *43*
descubierto,-a discovered *77*
descubrir to discover *43*
el descubrimiento discovery *46*
desde from *80*
desear to wish, desire *23*
desembarcar to disembark, unload *139*
la despedida goodbye *37*
despellejado,-a skinned *98*
el despertador alarm clock *76*
despertar (ie) to awaken *76*
después afterward *70*
el destino destination *37*
la destrucción destruction *131*
destruir to destroy *44*
detrás de behind *98*
el día day *12*
el dialecto dialect *139*
devolver to bring back *127*
el diario diary *12*
dibujar to draw *10*
el diccionario dictionary *35*
el diente tooth *13*
diferente different *37*
la dificultad difficulty *122*
la dimensión dimension *92*
el dinero money *78*
el dios god *22*

la diosa goddess 22
dirigir to direct 80
el diseño design 115
divertido,-a fun, amusing 77
el dólar dollar 76
dominar to dominate 134
el domingo Sunday 39
donde where 44
¿dónde? where? 6
dormir to sleep 33
 dormir como un lirón sleep
 like a log 111
dos two 102
dramático,-a dramatic 81
dulce sweet 127
durante during 36

E

la edad age 37
el edificio building 59
el ejemplo example 5
el elefante elephant 134
elegante elegant 58
el embarcadero dock 119
la emergencia emergency 42
emocionante exciting 2
empacar to pack 134
emparejar to match 20
empinado,-a high, lofty 135
emplumado,-a feathered 135
en busca de in search of 2
encantar to delight, enchant 58
encerrar (ie) to enclose 30
encima on top 114
encontrar (ue) to find 46
enfermo,-a sick 29
enfrente de in front of 53
enorme huge 13
enormemente extremely 69
entero,-a entire 36
enterrar (ie) to bury 87
la entrada entrance 127
entrar to enter 44
entre between 22
entusiasmado,-a enthusiastic 2
entusiasmo enthusiasm 2
la envidia envy 47

la época epoch 43
el equipaje baggage 70
el equipo equipment 30
la escalera stairway 30
el escalofrío chill 131
el escalón stair step 130
la esclavitud slavery 119
esconder to hide 25
escribir to write 12
escrito written 45
el, la escritor,-a writer 45
el escritorio desk 45
la escritura writing 45
escuchar to listen 11
 ¡Escúchenme! Listen to me! 92
la escuela school 75
el escultor sculptor 115
el esfuerzo effort 71
eso that 86
el espacio space 49
la espalda back 114
espantoso,-a terrifying 139
especial special 115
especialmente especially 69
esperar to hope, wait for 13
espiritual spiritual 131
espléndido,-a magnificent 58
la esposa wife 53
el esqueleto skeleton 30
estar to be 8
la estaca stake 110
estacionar to park 110
la estatua statue 46
estimular to stimulate 59
estos,-as these 58
el estómago stomach 135
estrecho,-a narrow 118
la estructura structure 115
el, la estudiante student 51
eterno,-a eternal 131
la evidencia evidence 135
evitar to avoid 119
la exclamación exclamation 41
exclamar to exclaim 2
exhibir to exhibit 93
existir to exist 126
exótico,-a exotic 1

explicar to explain *2*
el, la explorador,-a explorer *8*
explorar to explore *114*
la expresión expression *1*
extático,-a ecstatic *47*
extincto,-a extinct *118*
el, la extranjero,-a foreigner *139*
extraño,-a strange *2*
el extraterrestre
    extraterrestrial *49*

F

fabuloso,-a fabulous *92*
la fachada facade *134*
la familia family *8*
famoso,-a famous *30*
el fantasma ghost *86*
fantástico,-a fantastic *1*
fascinante fascinating *43*
feliz happy *86*
feroz ferocious *1*
fértil fertile *104*
el festival festival *127*
festivo,-a festive *98*
la figura figure *131*
la fila line, row *105*
   fila india single file *105*
físico,-a physical *131*
flaco,-a thin *37*
la flor flower *59*
flotante floating *71*
la flotilla flotilla *139*
Folklórico (el Ballet) Folklore
    dances *92*
el fondo bottom, depths *30*
la forma shape *26*
la fortaleza fort *138*
el fósforo match *33*
la foto photo *12*
la frase sentence *70*
frenético,-a frenzied *110*
fresco,-a cool, fresh *98*
el frijol bean *111*
la fruta fruit *98*
el frutal fruit tree *104*
el fuego fire *21*

la fuente fountain *58*
fuera outside *64*
fuerte strong *13*
funcionar to function, work *111*
el futuro future *1*

G

la gallina hen *58*
el gallo rooster *64*
ganar to win, to earn *75*
garantizar to guarantee *87*
la garganta throat *98*
la garrapata tick *111*
la garra claw *13*
la garza heron *119*
el gato montés mountain
    lion *118*
generalmente generally *96*
el gentío crowd *36*
la glorieta (de tráfico) traffic
    circle *104*
gobernar (ie) to govern *126*
el gobierno government *80*
golpear to beat, strike *25*
gordo,-a fat *37*
gracias thanks *53*
grande large *18*
la grandeza grandeur *134*
grano de oro nugget of gold,
    tidbit of information *125*
el Grijalvo river in Sumidero
    Canyon *119*
gritar to shout *2*
el grito shout, outcry *25*
la gruta cave *119*
el guajolote turkey *104*
el guardacostas Coast Guard
    cutter *61*
el guardapolvo dust cover,
    apron *61*
el guardarropa wardrobe,
    closet *61*
la guerra war *39*
el, la guía guide *119*
gustar to like, be pleasing to *11*
el gusto taste *59*

H

haber to have *97*
habitar to inhabit *86*
hablar to talk *90*
hacer to make, to do *12*
hacia toward *127*
la hamaca hammock *32*
la hambre hunger *16*
la hamburguesa hamburger *111*
harto,-a fed up *92*
hasta up to, until *122*
hay there is, there are *2*
hecho de made from *114*
las heriditas cuts and bruises *24*
el hermano brother *8*
el hielo ice *98*
la hierba herb *126*
el hierro iron *24*
el, la hijo,-a son, daughter *92*
hipnótico,-a hypnotic *127*
la historia history *46*
el hogar home *131*
¡Hola! Hello! *71*
la hora hour *134*
el hornillo stove *33*
horroroso,-a terrifying *24*
hoy today *80*
la huelga strike *81*
la huella track *139*
el hueso bone *115*
el huevo egg *80*
el huipil Indian blouse *122*
Huitzilopochtli Mayan god of war *86*
humano,-a human *87*
el humo smoke *126*
húmedo,-a damp, moist *130*

I

la idea idea *24*
la identidad identity *59*
identificar to identify *14*
la iglesia church *86*
la iguana iguana *98*
iluminar to light *127*

ilustrar to illustrate *81*
imaginar to imagine *13*
el impacto impact *46*
el imperio empire *86*
imponer to impose *140*
impresionante impressive *81*
el incienso incense *126*
inclinar to slant *135*
increíble incredible *87*
el, la indio,-a Indian *7*
indígena native *123*
inmediatamente immediately *71*
inmenso,-a immense *139*
inolvidable unforgettable *139*
la inscripción inscription *130*
el insecto insect *2*
insistir to insist *17*
interesante interesting *1*
interior interior *101*
internacional international *52*
interrumpir to interrupt *47*
intrépido,-a bold *29*
el invasor invader *138*
la inyección injection *35*

J

el jabalí wild boar *118*
el jade jade *131*
el jaguar jaguar *13*
el jardín garden *114*
la jaula cage *71*
el jefe chief *110*
el jején gnat *111*
el jeroglífico hieroglyphic *46*
el, la joven young person *71*
el juego game *115*
el jueves Thursday *39*
jugar to play *11*
el jugo juice *80*
julio July *89*

K

el kilómetro kilometer *115*
el kiosco kiosk *114*
Kukulcán Mayan god Quetzalcoatl *135*

L

los lacandones Mayan descendents *131*

el lado side *98*

la lancha launch *118*

la lanza spear *139*

largo,-a long *71*

el lavaplatos dishwasher *61*

la lápida cover *131*

leer to read *1*

el lema motto *24*

la lengua language, tongue *123*

levantarse to get up *114*

la libertad liberty *81*

libre free *114*

el libro book *36*

el limpiabotas bootblack *61*

el limpiachimeneas chimney sweep *61*

el limpiaparabrisas windshield wiper *61*

la linterna flashlight *24*

la lista list *30*

listo,-a ready *30*

loco,-a crazy *8*

el loro parrot *71*

la lucha fight *81*

el lugar place *110*

lujoso,-a luxurious *58*

luminoso,-a bright *122*

el lunes Monday *39*

LL

llameante flaming *139*

llamar to call *123*

la llave key *46*

la llegada arrival *139*

llegar to arrive *18*

llenar to fill *49*

llevar to carry, wear *19*

la lluvia rain *86*

M

magnífico,-a magnificent *80*

el maguey Yucatan cactus *134*

el maíz corn *88*

majestuoso,-a majestic *86*

mal de ojo evil eye *98*

la maleta suitcase *12*

el maletero porter *52*

la mano hand *99*

la mañana morning *76*

manejar to drive *106*

el mar sea *138*

maravilloso,-a wonderful *105*

la mariposa butterfly *119*

el martes Tuesday *39*

el martillo hammer *110*

más more *24*

la máscara mask *115*

matar to kill *139*

mayor older *77*

el mecapal forehead harness *114*

medicinal medicinal *126*

el medio middle *110*

mejor better *12*

melódico,-a melodic *76*

el, la mensajero,-a messenger *39*

el mercado market *89*

la mercancía merchandise *98*

el mes month *102*

meter to put in *99*

el metro meter *63*

el, la mexicano,-a Mexican *11*

el miedo fear *2*

mientras meanwhile *105*

el miércoles Wednesday *39*

el millón million *25*

la miniatura miniature *36*

mirar fijamente to stare *25*

la mirada glance *122*

misterioso,-a mysterious *1*

místico,-a mystical *127*

Mitla Mixtec ruin *114*

los mixtecas Mitla Indians *115*

moderno,-a modern *58*

mojado,-a wet *130*

la momia mummy *43*

el mono monkey *130*

montar to ride *139*

la montaña mountain *65*

montañoso,-a mountainous *118*

Monte Albán Zapotec city *115*
el montón pile, heap *123*
el monumento monument *115*
el mosaico mosaic *134*
mucho,-a much *18*
muerto,-a dead *43*
la multitud multitude *36*
el mundo world *2*
el mural mural painting *80*
la muralla wall *138*
el murciélago bat *8*
murieron (**morir**-Pret.) died *86*
murmurar murmur *25*
el museo museum *77*
muy very *2*
la música music *11*

N

Na-Bolom Mayan museum in San
    Cristóbal *123*
nadar to swim *110*
la navaja knife *12*
necesario,-a necessary *18*
necesitar to need *13*
negro,-a black *23*
ni neither, nor *24*
el, la niño,-a boy, girl *58*
la noche night *25*
¡No me digas! You don't say! *8*
nostálgico,-a nostalgic *139*
notar to notice *37*
la nube cloud *59*
nublado,-a cloudy *126*
nuestro,-a our *19*
nuevo,-a new *105*
el número number *115*

O

Oaxaca colonial city, center of
    Zapotec and Mixtec
    cultures *104*
el objeto object *18*
el obstáculo obstacle *104*
obvio,-a obvious *105*

el ocelote ocelot *118*
ocultar to conceal *15*
la ofrenda offering *86*
el oído hearing *59*
oir to hear *111*
¡Ojalá! Hopefully!, Here's
    hoping! *25*
¡Ojo! Look out! *7*
el ojo eye *13*
¡Olé! Bravo! *30*
el olfato smell *59*
el olor odor *59*
orgulloso,-a proud *46*
orgullosamente proudly *69*
la orilla bank *119*
el oro gold *115*
la oscuridad darkness *13*
oscuro,-a dark *25*
el oxígeno oxygen *76*

P

Pacal Mayan chieftain *130*
el paciente patient *127*
los padres parents *8*
pagar to pay *70*
el paisaje landscape *42*
el país country *59*
la paja straw *114*
el palacio palace *77*
Palenque Mayan site in
    Chiapas *30*
pálido,-a pale *98*
el palo stick *118*
palpitar to beat (heart) *135*
para for, in order to *12*
el paraíso paradise *86*
parar to stop *70*
parecer to appear *48*
la pared wall *80*
el parque park *59*
la parte part *80*
el pasaje ticket *35*
el, la pasajero,-a passenger *47*
el pasaporte passport *35*
pasar to spend (time) *93*
el patio patio, courtyard *58*

el **pedazo** piece *131*
peligroso,-a dangerous *2*
el **pelo** hair *131*
penetrar to penetrate *127*
la **península** peninsula *134*
pensar (ie) to think *84*
pequeño,-a small *58*
perder (ie) to miss (a plane) *30*
perdido,-a lost *43*
¡Perdóname! Pardon! Excuse
  me! *30*
perfecto,-a perfect *110*
la **perla** pearl *115*
permitir to permit *18*
el **perro** dog *58*
la **persona** person *37*
pesado,-a heavy *127*
el **peso** dollar *70*
el **pez** fish *65*
el **picaflor** hummingbird *61*
el **pie** foot *87*
la **piedra clave** keystone *46*
el **pino** pine tree *127*
pintado,-a painted *98*
pinturesco,a picturesque *100*
la **pirámide** pyramid *8*
la **pista** clue *46*
el **plan** plan *2*
planear to plan *12*
la **plataforma** platform *115*
el **plato** plate *135*
la **playa** beach *139*
la **pluma** feather *71*
poblado,-a populated *53*
pobre poor *131*
poder (ue) to be able to *46*
Pok-a-Tok Mayan ball game *115*
el **poncho** poncho, cape *122*
ponerse en camino to hit the
  road *92*
por ejemplo for example *5*
por eso therefore *86*
por favor please *37*
por fin finally *105*
¿por qué? why *18*
porque because *18*
practicar to practice *42*

precioso,-a valuable, pretty *123*
el **precipicio** cliff *119*
preferir (ie) to prefer *19*
la **pregunta** question *9*
preguntar to ask a question *12*
el **preparativo** preparation *11*
preparar to prepare *12*
la **presencia** presence *119*
la **presentación** presentation *92*
el **presidente** president *80*
prestar atención to pay
  attention *92*
primero,-a first *25*
la **prisa** hurry *16*
el **problema** problem *66*
el **producto** product *114*
profetizar to prophesy *138*
la **profundidad** depths *30*
profundo,-a deep *119*
pronto quickly *99*
propio,-a own *59*
la **protección** protection *13*
protestar to protest *64*
provocar to provoke *122*
el **pueblito** small village *104*
el **puente** bridge *86*
el **puesto** stall *123*
el **punto de vista** point of
  view *81*
purificar to purify *98*
puro,-a pure *104*
puso (se) (poner-Pret.) became *98*
púrpura purple *105*

Q

que that *13*
¿qué? what *6*
  ¡Qué barbaridad! How
    awful! *19*
  ¡Qué buena idea! What a good
    idea! *24*
  ¡Qué gentío! What a crowd! *41*
  ¡Qué horror! How horrible! *2*
  ¡Qué peligroso! How
    dangerous! *2*
querer (ie) to wish, to want *77*

el quetzal exotic jungle bird/god *83*

¿quién?, ¿quiénes? who *6*

quizás perhaps *98*

R

la radio radio *11*

la rama branch *127*

la rana frog *123*

rapidamente rapidly *70*

raro,-a rare *119*

el rascacielos skyscraper *59*

la raza race *37*

la razón reason *16*

el rebuzno braying *64*

el, la recepcionista receptionist *71*

el receptáculo receptacle *135*

recién recently *77*

recoger to pick up *93*

recomendar (ie) to recommend *71*

reconocer to recognize *139*

recto,-a straight *118*

el refresco soft drink *98*

refrescarse to refresh oneself *110*

regatear to bargain *123*

la región region, area *104*

reírse to laugh *25*

repetir (i) to repeat *70*

el, la representante representative *99*

respirar to breathe *71*

responder to respond *2*

el restaurante restaurant *77*

el resto rest *131*

resucitar to revive *43*

reunir to join *127*

revelar to reveal *30*

reverente respectful *87*

revivir to revive *44*

el revolucionario revolutionary *81*

rico,-a rich *111*

el río river *110*

la risa laughter *99*

Rivera, Diego famous Mexican painter *80*

rocoso,-a rocky *119*

rodear to surround *65*

rogar (ue) to beg *92*

rojo,-a red *98*

la ropa clothes *12*

ruidoso,-a noisy *76*

la ruina ruin *30*

la ruleta rusa Russian roulette *119*

la ruta route *118*

S

el sábado Saturday *39*

¿Sabes? Do you know? *4*

el sabor flavor *59*

sabroso,-a delicious *63*

el sacacorchos corkscrew *61*

sacar to take out *12*

sacar fotos to take pictures *12*

el sacerdote priest *127*

el saco sack, bag *33*

sacrificar to sacrifice *126*

el sacrificio sacrifice *87*

sagrado,-a sacred *135*

salir to leave *30*

saltar to jump *71*

saludar to greet *71*

salvaje savage *17*

la sangre blood *86*

sangriento,-a bloody *86*

sanguinario,-a bloodthirsty *86*

el, la santo,-a saint *123*

la sartén frying pan *24*

seco,-a dry *123*

secreto,-a secret *30*

secuestrar hijack *19*

seguir to follow *127*

seguro,-a sure *47*

según according to *38*

seis six *115*

la selva jungle *2*

la semana week *102*

sentar (ie) to sit *98*

el sentido sense *59*

sentir (ie) to feel 47
la señal signal, clue 52
el señor Mr., gentleman 12
la señora Mrs., Ms., lady 12
la señorita Miss 98
ser to be 28
la serpentina paper streamer 127
la serpiente snake 135
servir (i) to serve 15
si if 46
sí yes 25
siempre always 20
el siglo century 80
el símbolo symbol 134
sin without 99
la sinfonía symphony 76
siniestro,-a sinister 8
el sitio place 92
sobre on, about, over 36
sobrenatural supernatural 139
el sol sun 21
solamente only 44
el soldado soldier 87
sonar to sound 104
el sonido sound 59
la sonrisa smile 47
la sospecha suspicion 123
su, sus his, her, its, their, your 8
subir to get on, climb 37
subterráneo,-a subterranean 115
el suéter sweater 35
sufrir to suffer 65
sugerir (ie) to suggest 76
suicidarse to commit suicide 119
la superficie surface 119
la superstición superstition 123
el suroeste southeast 115
susurrar to whisper 131

T

el tacto touch 59
el talento talent 93
tallado,-a carved 115
también also 2
tan ... como as ... as 19
el tanque tank 33

tantos,-as so many 92
el tapir tapir 118
la tarántula tarantula 8
la tarde afternoon 29
la tarjeta card 35
el taxista taxi driver 64
el techo roof 122
la teja tile 122
tejer to weave 127
el tema theme 81
temblar (ie) to tremble 49
el templo temple 77
temprano early 134
tener (ie) to have 12
    tener calor to be hot 16
    tener cuidado to be careful 16
    tener frío to be cold 16
    tener hambre to be hungry 16
    tener miedo to be afraid 16
    tener prisa to be in a hurry 16
    tener razón to be right 16
    tener sueño to be sleepy 16
    tener suerte to be lucky 16
    tener ... años to be ... years
        old 16
terminar to end 138
la terraza terrace 49
el terremoto earthquake 49
el territorio territory 49
el, la terrorista terrorist 19
el tesoro treasure 8
el tiburón shark 98
el tiempo time 118
la tienda de campaña tent 33
la tierra earth, land 49
la tía aunt 2
típico,-a typical 105
Tlaloc god of rain 86
el tocadiscos record player 61
tocar to touch, to play (music) 59
todavía still 120
todo,-a all 12
    todo el mundo everyone 92
    todos los días every day 96
tomar to take 77
el tope speed bump 104
la tortilla flat, round bread 111

trabajar to work *94*
la tradición tradition *126*
el tráfico traffic *64*
el traje clothing, costume *105*
  el traje de baño bathing
    suit *111*
tranquilamente tranquilly *42*
transportar to transport *18*
tratar to try *123*
trece thirteen *20*
tres three *29*
triste sad *37*
la tristeza sadness *65*
la trompa elephant's trunk *134*
el trono throne *135*
el tulipero tulip tree *105*
Tulum Mayan fortress on east
  coast of Yucatan *135*
la tumba tomb *30*
la turquesa turquoise *127*
la túnica tunic *131*
turnar to take turns *118*
el tzotzil a Mayan language in
  Chiapas *123*

U

usar to use *115*
el utensilio utensil *33*
utilizar to use *115*
Uxmal Mayan site in
  Yucatan *134*

V

la vaca cow *104*
vagabundear to wander *111*
valiente brave *29*
el valle valley *30*
¡Vámonos! Let's go! *30*
variado,-a varied *104*
¡Vayan con Dios! Go with God! *70*
la vegetación vegetation *43*
la vela candle *33*
vender to sell *114*
venir (ie) to come *93*
la ventanilla window *42*

ver to see *12*
el verano summer *39*
la verdad truth *59*
verdadero,-a true, authentic *73*
verde green *105*
la verdura vegetable *104*
vestido,-a dressed *127*
el vestíbulo lobby *70*
la vez time *59*
viajar to travel *3*
el viaje the trip *2*
el, la viajero,-a traveler *36*
la víbora snake *111*
la víctima victim *65*
la vida life *43*
el viernes Friday *39*
viejo,-a old *98*
violento,-a violent *81*
visitar to visit *135*
la vista sight *59*
vivo,-a alive *87*
vivir to live *91*
vivito,-a y coleando alive and
  kicking *99*
volar (ue) to fly *63*
el volcán volcano *21*
volver to return *93*
la voz voice *46*
el vuelo flight *36*

Y

y and *2*
ya already *76*
Yaxchilán Mayan site of
  Bonampak murals and Lacandon
  worship *131*

Z

zambullirse to dive *138*
los zapotecas Indian builders of
  Monte Albán *115*
Zinacantán Indian village in
  Chiapas *126*
el zopilote vulture *104*
el Zócalo public square *76*

Grammar Index

qué, *41*

question words, *7*

reading strategies, *109*

related words, *63*

Roman mythology, days of the week from, *39*

ser, *29, 85*

subject pronouns, *51*

tener, expressions with, *17–21*

tierra, Latin root of, *49*

tortillas, different names for, *133*

ver, *85*

verbs
  -ar verbs, *85, 91*
  comer, *85, 91*
  endings, *51*
  -er verbs, *85, 91*
  estar, *29*
  hablar, *85, 91*
  ir, *85*
  -ir verbs, *85, 91*
  ser, *29, 85*
  tener, *17–21*
  ver, *85*
  vivir, *85, 91*
vivir, *85, 91*

week, days of the, *39*